Preface

Years ago, it occurred to me that change was happening quickly enough to suit lots of people. New technologies and lifestyle choices and values weren't catching on as quickly as they should. Climate change in the news, but not as much as it was in 2020, when COVID-19 somewhat pushed other subjects out of the spotlight for much of the year.

That doesn't make climate change less of a problem for the future. No. We obviously need to adapt to present climate realities as we try to mitigate future changes to the climate. We'll need a combination of new technologies, new economic policies, and cultural changes. We might have to transition to a lifestyle of eating less meat, or no meat, driving less, and living in smaller homes while we shift to using more renewable energy, recycle more, and cut our consumption across the board.

Even before climate change became something the general public talks about, there was the prospect of new and exciting technologies taking hold. New energy technologies like tide, wave, solar, and micro-hydro seemed mature enough to take over the world from fossil fuels and nuclear fission. Books like *Natural Capitalism* and *Cradle-to-Cradle* promised new ways to make things with less environmental harm.

But, how does a person or group or coalition of groups help these sorts of innovations catch on? That's the question. Maybe this book is part of the answer.

This is not just a book about selling revolutionary green technologies or processes. I was focused on that sort of thing in the beginning, back in the early 2000s.

As a sociologist, I have also learned a few things about designing and selling social innovations.

Later, I learned even more by reading books on creativity, problem analysis, strategy, and decision making. Some of that reading is condensed and organized here.

This book represents years of reading, writing, and research on tools we can
use to create new and better ideas, sell our ideas to the people who need them, evaluate our ideas, analyze our options, look at challenges and opportunities in a rational, systematic way and in short, make our organizations and our social change efforts more effective and more efficient.

Effectiveness of course means that you are accomplishing what you meant to do. You meet or exceed monthly goals for your fund-raising efforts. Your movement passes new worker protection laws or recycling laws. Efficiency means the time and money you invest to reach those goals. If you get the same buy-in for voluntary recycling with only 75% of the work wouldn't that be cool? If you could could get 60% of small businesses to join a program, instead of your goal of 50%, that would be a big win.

Part 1:
A Social Innovation System

1 – Who Needs a New System?

Good order is the foundation of all things – Edmund Burke

You know the headlines: Climate change is a threat to civilization. Mass extinctions are in progress, global poverty, religious extremism, economic inequality, health care for all, mandatory recycling, and so on. Racism is a massive problem. The Whatever your cause, problem, or challenge, there is always a way to get better results with whatever resources you have on hand. If you want to change people not just systems or rules, promoting vegetarian or vegan diets or science literacy or whatever, you can always use a new promotional idea? Fundraising always calls for market research, hard work, and creative thinking. Innovation may not be crucial in fundraising but it sure can help. Right? Right.

And, the bigger the change, the more dramatic the change, the faster you want to go, the more you need to hustle. But that won't work. You also need a better system for organizing your work, studying your audience, generating ideas, and so on.

In other words, you need a system that supports effective analysis, brainstorming and decision making. This chapter introduces the system. The rest of the book explains the components of the system and teaches you to apply them. Let me start by reviewing some assumptions and assertions that are not too controversial.

Some Truisms About the Social Sector

Nonprofits need to be more effective and efficient. All nonprofits need to be careful of how they use time and money. The new fiscal climate in the developed world does not allow for ineffective programs and inefficient use of donors' money.

Grant-making organizations reward innovative project ideas with money, as long as the organization is effective. Innovative projects need to be creative, obviously, but also aimed at solving real problems in ways that make sense for the setting. Those two points might seem self-evident but need some explaining.

Needs and demands don't always line up, for a few reasons. The "need equals demand" fallacy may be the main contributor to that mismatch between what people want and what nonprofits actually do. You may sense a need for more more recycling locations and go out to try and secure resources to buy bins and keep the community informed about your project. One year later, after over 1,000 hours of unpaid labor you have three conveniently located bins that hardly anyone uses. Why? Because convenient recycling isn't what people needed. What they needed was better information on why recycling their glass and plastic is important. Only a handful of recycling devotees appreciate the bins, and they did succeed in recruiting a few users among friends and family.

The bandwagon effect may be in play as well. Causes rise and fall in prominence or urgency. The COVID-19 pandemic closed and ultimately killed lots of businesses, driving an increased demand for help from food banks. Climate change rises to prominence during a bad hurricane season. A high-profile case or a major campaign by a huge foundation raises the profile of domestic violence in the United States. Money and media attention flow in the directions indicated in all three cases. That new attention can take money and volunteers away from any number of other worth causes.

Chasing money might be another factor in this gap between need and demand. The higher profile the problem or the cause, the easier it can be to earn big donations or win a grant. This is good news fro you if you are responsible for keeping your nonprofit funded. However, this side effect of the bandwagon approach leads nonprofit staff to mis-allocate their resources.

A Partial Solution

What if you started off by exploring your challenge and your own assumptions. Might you have concluded that the problem is consumption or ingorance. If you decide that people consume too much stuff, and that is why they generate so much waste that needs recycling, you might dismiss recycling as not too important. But, how could you possibly convince people to consume less. Who wants to be told they need to buy less stuff, much less stuff? No one cares really, maybe you'll convert a few people who are interested in minimalism but were not ready to make the leap into this new lifestyle until they encountered your marketing. More realistically, you'll need to come up with some creative tricks. Lateral thinking is a must!

Sometimes defining the problem is a problem. Having a system to explore your thinking and knowledge about a challenge can help. Many social problems are difficult to define. Is poverty really caused by the country's capitalist economic system? If so, then capitalism is the problem. Can a single NGO, no matter how effective really replace cause capitalism to be replaced with socialism or communism? No. But, if you are convinced that capitalism itself is the problem, you can be sidetracked by efforts to do something that's not realistically achievable.

If you redefine the problem as being the way capitalism is practiced, then you can look for a specific problem that's solvable.

Taking a different approach to defining problems and their symptoms is going to be needed for nonprofits to make the best use of tighter resources. This book provides some of the tools you need to take that philosophical statement and make it concrete. New tools and techniques to support social activism will make solving that newly-defined problem more realistic.

What about nonprofits that aren't dedicated to solving social problems? Lots of art organizations, historical societies, and education charities aren't trying to solve a big problem like climate change or extreme poverty. Yet, those organizations still could benefit from a novel approach to raising money, or creating new programs. Community development organizations, arts organizations, non-profit theaters, museums, and non-profit hospitals need new program ideas, new fundraising methods, and new marketing techniques. A systematic approach to finding good new ideas will help overcome the constant challenges of engaging with people and getting donations.

And what about organizations that are dedicated to solving the big problems that the world faces. Climate change, overpopulation, water shortages and other big, global problems call for innovation in social marketing, policy, and program development. Of course, some non-profits work on technical innovations that can ameliorate one or more of those big global problems. A method for generating viable new ideas will be useful.

Other organizations work to solve many other social problems. What can we do when society seems to be broken? What can we do about the many challenges facing societies around the world? Many opportunities for improving the world, as opposed to simply fixing a problem, clearly exist.

Global climate change is a looming disaster that we probably aren't doing enough about. Drug abuse is a plague on many communities. Progressive social policy ideas aren't wildly popular, or sometimes even a little bit popular.

Nonprofits devote tons of time to marketing and communication. Sometimes those efforts are wildly successful, but usually not. Any fundraising, marketing, or public relations effort that's not a hit could be improved next time, with the right approach. Before the project even starts, a little analysis can improve the idea, and verify that the likely results are likely to justify the cost in time and money.

In many ways, our efforts to make society better in some way do come up short, or take too long, or fall flat. Maybe we can't get enough signatures on a petition or raise enough money. We see chances to do more but lack the resources to exploit those opportunities. All those challenges can be handled, if you know the right techniques.

Hundreds of thousands of people in social service organizations, schools, and activist groups of all types know that their organizations can do more. Maybe your organization needs to raise more money, recruit more volunteers, or get better outcomes for clients. Social entrepreneurs know that new ideas are needed – programs, projects, organizations need to be created and funded. Schools need new programs and policies.

Activists and nonprofit executives need to solve problems, exploit opportunities, and make good decisions. Informal methods like "brainstorming" work well enough. Experience and some basic logic often lead to a solution for a sticky problem. An unstructured process leads to sound decisions some of the time. Maybe the true consequences of a less-than-thorough decision process are just hard to identify.

Government agencies need to cope with budget cuts and constant demands to be more effective or efficient. Creative thinking and disciplined decision making can help. Where government programs are not performing up to expectations, creative thinking and systematic problem-solving tools can yield real improvements.

Anyone who can relate to the previous paragraphs will learn a few things in *The Creative Activist*. Educators and education administrators will find out how to create new policies and programs. Nonprofit managers will learn how to create innovative programs, policies, projects, and fundraisers. They'll also find ways to sell ideas, recruit people, and compensate for a lack of funds.

Social entrepreneurs will learn how to develop better approaches to dealing with their chosen issue. Anyone else whose interested in promoting socially responsible business will find ways to develop better products, services, policies, business processes, and marketing.

Writers and consultants have created many powerful techniques for solving problems and exploiting opportunities. Everyone has heard of brainstorming, and most of us have done it before. Most activists and other social conscious types aren't aware of the many better idea-generating options that exist. Ditto for ways to study social problems and understand them.

This is a book about nonprofit effectiveness, as well as being a book about generating great ideas. Effectiveness requires making sound decisions about what ideas will work under a particular set of circumstances. Some challenges require some formal investigation or problem analysis, so you can figure out just what to be innovative about. Creativity doesn't always require that you go with a completely new idea; there probably is no such thing anyway. Stealing ideas is allowed and encouraged!

Preparing for Social Change Efforts

Working to improve society is a difficult task even if all the stars align and everyone likes you. People disagree about what the problem is, or about whether there is a problem at all. Sometimes people disagree on what to do. What if people disagree with your idea of an "improvement?" A ban on handgun ownership would count as progress to some but that doesn't make it progress to everyone! The causes of a social problem are often poorly understood or not understood at all. Ideological or religious explanations of social phenomena gloss over the real complexities of the social world. No matter what side of any environmental debate you are on, you probably have seen ideology trump science. In our enthusiasm to make positive things happen we might simply assume our idea is a good one, because we want it to be good.

Creating change requires knowledge, commitment, flexibility, and accurate information. You had better be passionate about a cause to withstand the opposition, the indifference, the bureaucratic garbage, and the financial challenges. Besides that, all decision making is emotional; we can only use formal tools or techniques to clarify our thinking and guide our emotions. Reason, the application of means-ends thinking to support action based on our values, will help ensure that our energies are being put to good use within whatever arena we want to apply ourselves. Trying to change society in any way needs a plan. Setting off on a well-meaning crusade to do something about some problem is not a reasonable substitute for making an actual plan.

The Power of a System

You recognize the need for new ideas, or at least the need to do a better job of selling ideas that already exist. *Creating Change* assembles the information readers can use to help create viable new ideas, implement the ideas, or sell the ideas to others.

Many books and Web sites describe techniques for innovation, idea generation, problem solving, or decision making. Most of the material is written for people in business. To a certain extent this makes perfectly good sense. People in businesses are under pressure to develop new products, new services, and new markets. Of course, nonprofits are also under pressure to raise funds from various sources, to improve their operating efficiency, and to develop new programs. Some of the same pressures exist in government and education as well. Previous authors have still focused on business because that is where the biggest easy-to-reach market can be found. They assume, with some justification, that readers will be able to translate what they read into the nonprofit, education, and government settings where those readers work.

No single book has ever presented a comprehensive set of "thinking tools" and shown how they could be applied in the nonprofit world. This is what *Creating Change* does. You can learn to use techniques for problem solving, idea generation, idea evaluation, decision analysis, and structured problem solving. You can learn how to apply those tools to all of the challenges that face social sector organizations: fund raising, social marketing, program design, advertising, and troubleshooting issues with policies and programs.

Problem solving, opportunity exploitation, and the selling of ideas are important parts of the innovation process. It should be obvious that problems need to be solved because they are problems. This focus on problem solving is understandable but a bit negative. Opportunities to do more, sell ideas more effectively, raise more money, create better programs, and generally to be more effective are just waiting to be taken advantage of.

People often neglect opportunity thinking for two reasons. Finding and exploiting opportunities is both risky and a distraction from the necessary routines of the workplace. Even worse, there may be a steady stream of problems that demand one's attention. The same issues exist in community groups, in government agencies, in nonprofits, and in schools.

Most organizations could be more effective if more opportunities could be identified and acted upon. Where do you find the time and money and expertise? How do you identify the opportunities and weigh their value to your organization? How do you evaluate the potential impacts of things you could/should do in the future? What do you do about the potential and undesirable consequences that accompany any future course of action?

How do you weigh the costs of acting on an opportunity versus doing something else? Businesses often evaluate these "opportunity costs" in lost revenue, and profits, and market share. Nonprofits also need to generate revenue through grants, donors, corporate sponsors, silent auctions, bake sales, calendar sales and 101 other fund raising activities. Nonprofits also need to have an impact on the community/nation/world through programs, services, advocacy, research, and public education efforts. So, nonprofit managers have to ask the question "What could we be doing instead and what impact would that choice have made?" Sometimes the question gets asked and answered at an unconscious level and sometimes you don't have to answer the question because you are simply put in charge of an existing program.

Senior staff and boards of directors and entrepreneurial staff still need to ask questions about the opportunity costs of their organization's efforts. What is the cost of not doing X instead of Y or Z? Sometimes we know, or can make a reasonable judgment based on years of formal education and experience. Sometimes, and even most of the time when the stakes are really high, it would be nice to have a formal process for evaluating opportunity costs and cost-benefit ratios and other operational factors in decisions on how to deploy the organization's funds, staff, and volunteers.

Deciding How to Invest Time and Money

Ineffective efforts still use up the organization's resources, Do you know how much effort and money you invest in bringing people to your Web site? Do you know how much time you invest in Facebook every month? What else could your staff and volunteers be doing to raise money or generate awareness of your organization? The effort that's not going into those activities represents the opportunity cost of what you are doing now.

Knowing the likely benefits and costs of implementing a new idea is crucial to making good fundraising and marketing decisions. If you are starting from zero, you need to assess how much time and money different communication tactics will cost. You also need to consider the likely results of using that tactic. Will the benefits outweigh the cost?

If you have a development or communications strategy now,

take some time to evaluate it: Write down each marketing and
fundraising activity your organization engages in. Do you have a
Facebook page? Note how many hours a month you spend using
Facebook to connect with people. If you put on an event to raise money
and awareness, that event cost money, staff time, and volunteer time.
What was the total investment in your last event? You should end up
with a list that looks like this (yours may be neater or messier):

1. Facebook presence – 20 hours per month and $360 for staff
   time.
2. July 4 fundraising party – 80 hours of staff time(costing $1920),
   120 hours of volunteer time, $1500
3. Web hosting and updating - $15/month (hosting), 8 hours of
   volunteer time per month
4. Labor Day fundraiser – 40 hours of staff time (costing $960),
   10 hours of volunteer time

As you look at new fundraising and marketing ideas, you will
want to evaluate how many hours it will take and how much money
needs to be invested. An idea that sounds great at first might take 100
hours and $1,000 to implement. That's fine when you can realistically
make far more than $1,000. But, what if you can't count on doing so
well?

You also need to realistically evaluate the likely results of
implementing your ideas. Consider a fundraising idea that involves
collecting old electronics to recycle them If you invest 100 hours of
staff and volunteer time and $1,000 for advertising and supplies is the
idea a good one? What if you estimate that the event can only generate
$2,000 to $3,000 in donations? If you don't calculate the investment
and estimate the return you can waste resources.

That unpleasant business term "cost-benefit analysis" that

makes some liberal activists cringe has to be taken seriously. How can you do a cost-benefit analysis on helping inner-city kids overcome the many problems that can keep them from having happy, productive adult lives? My response is that you must do a cost-benefit analysis that covers money, staff time, and volunteer efforts. Why? I assume that you want to help as many inner-city kids as possible with the resources that you have available. Cost-benefit analysis does not have to be a cold, rational analysis of what efforts shall continue and what shall end. Instead, you can use a formal analysis of how you are using the organization's resources to evaluate the effectiveness of your work and to make plans for the future. People will, probably, thank you in the end for thinking about how to do the most good with whatever resources you have.

The same logic applies to advocacy, program design, and so forth. How much are you getting for your investment? Until you know that, you won't know whether your resources are being put to the best possible use.

Getting Ideas

Generating ideas can be easy. You just concentrate on a certain objective or topic or issue and record whatever ideas come to mind. In fact this is a reasonable creative technique. Simple concentration can yield a decent *quantity* of ideas, some good *quality* ideas, and some *evaluation criteria*. You may even come to question whether you are focusing your creative efforts on the correct subject. Using some relatively more complicated brainstorming techniques can improve your thinking on the target for your creative efforts, your standard for what counts as a good idea, your ability to generate ideas, and even the quality of the ideas.

You should also evaluate ideas in a systematic way. You have to know what constraints in resources, cultural norms, technology, time, and influence will mean in terms of restricting the ideas you can realistically sell or implement. Bring relevant assumptions out in the open and see if they really hold up. You might dismiss an idea based on some assumption that might hold elsewhere, or maybe made sense in general a couple of years ago. Now, however, that assumption does not apply. If you had stuck by it, you would have tossed out a great idea.

Evaluation can become too subjective. Of course the act of evaluating ideas is subject to emotion, bias, and personal tastes. The point is to use a method that forces us to systematically consider ideas relative to explicit evaluation criteria. If you've taken another look at your assumptions, you can take a few more minutes to identify your evaluation criteria. How exactly will you answer the question "What counts as a good idea?" Only then can our emotions be applied most effectively. As Edward De Bono once wrote "The purpose of thinking is to so arrange the world that the application of our emotions will give satisfactory results."

Nonprofit managers, government officials, activists, and educators often have to make decisions about how best to use their people and money and time. Sometimes an informal analysis and discussion will reveal what needs to be done. Maybe some data collection and analysis is called for before the decision point is reached. In any case, this sort of relatively unstructured and informal decision analysis may not be adequate. You may want to have a formal method for prioritizing use of resources or for evaluating the potential outcome of a decision or of weighing the merits of available alternatives. In those situations you will need to use formal methods of decision analysis. While decision science is quite complicated, a couple of relatively easy techniques exist. You can readily learn them with a bit of practice and start to apply them in your organization. *Creating Change* will teach you how to do that.

What Not to Do

Being determined to plan, analyze, and brainstorm effectively will help to head off some of this social betterment problems:

1. Wait for inspiration. Professional writers can't afford to do this. You have to decide when to generate new ideas, then you need to get to work.

2. Criticize the government for what it is doing, or not doing.

3. Promote half-baked ideas that promote vague "goals" like social justice or corporate responsibility.

4. Assume you know what the problem is and how to solve it.

5. Criticize 'the system" or some part of it (the patriarchy, corporate cronyism, et cetera).

6. Assume the problem NEEDS a new idea. Sometimes the old ideas are fine, it is just the marketing or the implementation that needs working on.

7. Follow trends in activism. Deciding what to do based on what' popular is easy – makes you look more serious and makes it a little easier to raise money – but risks diverting resources from other aspects of a problem, other populations, or other geographic areas.

Waiting for inspiration to strike won't work and may end in

disaster. You obviously can't wait for inspiration to visit if you have a deadline. Everyone has targets and deadlines on the job. If you are working outside of an organization, you still need to set goals that have deadlines.

Social criticism is fine but it has a time and a place. The point is to know that a specific criticism is justifiable. Organizing a protest march or a die-in or whatever may be a waste of time unless you have a larger plan with concrete goals and deadlines.

Criminal justice reform is a concept, not a plan or even a goal. Do you want the local government to implement Reform A and Reform B? Fine. Have you worked out the best way to get those reforms up for a vote or whatever the next step is. Create a plan by doing a little thought experiment or running a scenario or doing some research. How have other activist groups gotten something like Reform A and B passed. Can you copy some or all of their methodology. Has there ever been a return-on-investment analysis to show that demonstrations and rallies do anything that justifies the time and money invested? Complaints, advertised, are not interesting or helpful. Inspiration usually only comes to those who work at it. As author Jack London said, "You can't wait for inspiration. You have to go after it with a club."

Trying to get creative isn't always the best idea. Sometimes, you have a perfectly good system or plan or process. You just need to use it. Try to avoid being edgy and "innovative" because that is what gets attention on social media.

Following trends can be a problem in many ways. There's a good reason why the "bandwagon" approach to things gets lots of criticism. It might be okay to do something because that's what other environmental charities are doing, but you have to consider your own organization's goals, resources, and social environment. You may also be assuming, without cause, that Big Organization, knows their trendy tactics work. Their decision makers could be a victim of their own thinking or of trends in the nonprofit sector *they* haven't studied.

Five Social Innovation Principles

In a way, this book can be called a prescriptive work that's promoting a rational approach to social betterment. "Creating Change," to coin a term, has five characteristics:

1. *Opportunity Thinking* – Look for ways to obtain new resources, make new alliances, or make more of an impact..

2. *Think Scientifically* – Use data, systematic observations, and formal analytical tools to understand the current situation and the impacts of your own efforts. Don't let terms like "empirical" and "formal" disturb you; the concepts aren't hard to apply.

3. *Look for Leverage* – Look for ways to attack a social problem that will give the best results for your resources. In other words, look for places to intervene or act where you can get maximum value for your time and money.

4. *Be Systematic* – Use a system to structure and explore challenges, create evaluation criteria for ideas, generate ideas, evaluate ideas, decide what to do, and monitor results. Again, this is not as complicated as it might seem.

5. *Adopt a Marketing Mindset* – Think of yourself as being in sales or advertising, with your services or ideas being "sold" to benefit people.

   Creating Change gives *you* the basic tools you need for all five parts of Creating Change. Think of this book as a complete system that you can use. Use the resources provided at the end of many chapters to acquire specialized knowledge or a skill that's too advanced for an introductory book like this one. Or, skim through *Creating Change* and pick out the tools and techniques that seem most immediately applicable in your situation.

The Toolkit rests on two other principles that are, perhaps, ignored by too many activists. First, we should work from past and present behaviors to predict what will probably happen in the future. It is no use to think about things people should do or how people should be, or could be. Second, we should assume that people are behaving reasonably given their priorities, perceptions, attitudes, beliefs, cultural background, and social environment. People are only stupid from a perspective that is disconnected from the real context in which the "stupid people" are living out their lives.

Everyone needs to be sold on a new way of acting or thinking or living. Why would it be any other way? We all have our own concerns, interests, and priorities in life. Unless you can help us solve some problem that we see as a problem, you might need to do a good bit of marketing. The same observation applies to voting for something; why do it if there is no problem?

Charles McCoy, author of *Why Didn't I Think of That?*, offers four principles to keep in mind during any problem-solving effort. Anticipating problems, or opportunities, is a critical to effective planning. Potential Problem/Potential Opportunity Analysis and Consequence and Sequel are two effective tools for identifying future problems and opportunities. The Phoenix Checklist can also help you anticipate future circumstances. McCoy lists other some simple and powerful steps we can take to anticipate events:

1. Think the unthinkable

2. Expect the unexpected

3. Consider both the significance and likelihood of consequences

4. Invite and value blistering criticism – but make sure it's constructive criticism and not just general complaining or criticizing: "This will never work!"

Give your imagination a chance to break free by thinking about what you could do without limits imposed by money, skill, connections, and so forth. While none of your wild imaginings might be useful in the real world, some of those thoughts might lead to practical ideas. Take notes.

Expecting the unexpected means being open to the reality that new risks and opportunities will emerge as you work. To make things a bit more practical, consider that any policy, program, marketing effort, or fundraising plan presents lots of ways that unanticipated problems and opportunities. Take some time to think about the potential risks in any new project or program. Write down those risks. Repeat the process for opportunities.

You may have identified some consequence of an idea and their likelihood when you looked for risks and opportunities. Take some more time to consider what might come from implementing the idea. This part is optional for some types of ideas, but crucial to policies and programs. Consequence and Sequel, a tool created by creative thinking expert Edward De Bono, offers a simple framework for thinking about the consequences of implementing an idea. Chapter X describes how to use Consequence and Sequel.

Criticism might be unpleasant, but failure is even more unpleasant. Early criticisms can head off trouble, which saves the organization time and money. If group feedback isn't practical, at least run your idea past a few people. Don't use the easy and obvious group of people.

The Seven Steps of Social Innovation

A process needs steps, even when you know that not all of the steps need to be followed every time. This new process for Systematic Social Innovation has seven steps:

1. *Analyze Challenges* – question assumptions and ask plenty of questions
2. *Study Your Environment* – the social environment, goals, and objectives need to be considered
3. *Define "Good Idea"* – look at many sources of information and ideas for anything you can use
4. *Think Creatively* –use brainstorming techniques or systematic idea generation methods
5. *Evaluate and Improve Ideas* – use objective criteria and a system for picking a winner or winners
6. *Implement* – Put the idea into practice as a fundraiser, ad campaign, whatever
7. *Evaluate and Adjust* – test hypotheses; relate parts of the problem/issue to the whole.

This book focuses on steps 1 through 5 of the process. Implementation and evaluation/adjustment get plenty of attention in other books and articles. The point in the pages that follow is to share tools and techniques that any social innovator or activist could use at each of the first five steps.

Solving the Problem

Problem solving and idea generation usually go together. You want a solution to your problem and need new ideas so you turn to brainstorming to generate ideas. But, what about determining the cause of the problem? How do you do that? Coming up with creative approaches to a symptom of a problem or something that has no relationship to the problem is just a waste of time and resources. Don't jump to conclusions about the cause of a problem.

In this book, a problem is a deviation from expected performance, when the cause for the deviation is unknown. This definition comes from *The New Rational Manager* by Charles H. Kepner and Benjamin B. Tregoe. In activism then, a problem exists where the expected performance of some part of society is not what we want, for reasons that are undetermined. Lack of universal health care is not a problem, because the a problem can't be stated in the form of a solution. You would need to frame the problem this way: "Why is there not a universal healthcare system of any type in the United States?" If you think this way, you will stand a good chance of finding a cause that can be worked on. Simply advocated for universal health care to solve the "problem" of universal health care not existing is, well, not real problem solving at all.   Later in this book you'll learn some not-too-difficult ways to systematically investigate the causes of problems in your community or organization or society.

Different challenges call for different tools. Fundraising is a creative challenge. Poorer than expected results from a program need to be examined through some form of structured problem analysis. Figuring out how to influence more people with a message is a creative challenge. Creating a new program or policy is involves problem analysis and brainstorming new ideas. Of course, when you've identified the best approach to a problem, an approach that can be embodied in a new policy or program, you have to evaluate your ideas. You may have multiple workable ideas that need to be compared. Maybe you have a potentially workable idea that needs to be refined in some way. This is the most likely outcome of a creative thinking challenge - one or more ideas that need to be refined.

Social betterment is *not* about solving problems and only solving problems. Sometimes everything is OK but we see a chance to do better. The schools can be improved cheaply if the school board would do X. We could make the city even more attractive by doing Y, which won't take that much time or money by the way. "Selling" improvements to things that don't need to be "fixed" can be a formidable challenge in itself. Our minds are primed by evolution to look for problems that pose an immediate threat, so we tend to quickly lose interest in anything that's not a problem.

Everyone in the social sector looks for, or wishes for, better ways to cope with challenges. Civilization as a whole has problems. Global climate change comes to mind. Then there is AIDS, malaria, global poverty, ethnic cleansing, water shortages, and an urbanization crisis in many developing countries. Other challenges are much smaller and closer to home: getting the city to spruce up some parks, convincing people to care more about local government, raising money for a high-school trip to Europe, or fighting censorship. *Creating Change* offers simple techniques that can help your organization tackle challenges of all sizes.

Activists obviously care about those sorts of challenges. But activism is also about pursuing opportunities, or so one hopes. Why not use your time, money, and skills to seize on some opportunity. Maybe you see a chance to get more people interested in using renewable energy sources for their homes. Maybe you can see a realistic way to reduce traffic. Some big media event may offer a change to get people more interested in locally grown, organic food.

How will you take advantage of such opportunities? You have to recognize opportunities, then you need to have an idea or two, and you need to decide exactly how to proceed. Sometimes not much creativity or analysis seems called for; creativity and analysis can still be helpful. Other opportunities are bigger or more complicated so more resources will be needed. In those cases some creativity and formal analysis of the situation certainly seems warranted. *Creating Change* offers tools you can use in either case.

How to Use This Book

What can you look forward to learning? What level of detail will you find? Can you really learn enough from one book to be more creative, solve problems more effectively, and make better decisions? The short answer is "no." You cannot learn all of those things, all you need to know, from one book. What you can get from *Creating Change* is an understanding of some tools and techniques that you can practice with then use effectively. Practice has to precede actual use. If you want to make really efficient use of your time think of a problem or opportunity that faces you or your organization as you read this book. Follow along with the advice and instructions, answering questions as you go.

Creating Change is supposed to be interactive. Try the exercises you'll find here. As soon as you identify some interesting resources, from the lists at the end of most chapters, go to the library or the Internet and do something. Download a trial copy of some software.

Order a book from Amazon.com. Talk to your friends and coworkers about tools, techniques, challenges, and opportunities. Take a class. You'll find information on classes and workshops in several chapters.

Creating Change has ideas for student activists, individuals who aren't part of a group, and all school or nonprofit employees. A student activist will learn some simple and free ways to develop, implement, or sell ideas for campus projects and community projects, including unique fundraisers and consciousness-raising exercises. A lone activist should really be trying to connect with other like-minded individuals. Creating Change contains directions on stealing ideas, on solo brainstorming, and on selling ideas to others. A nonprofit staffer or school employee, regardless of their role, can expect to find techniques for creating or improving programs, projects, and operations.

Creating Change covers a wide range of tools and techniques. You'll learn about tools that were developed for businesses to use in solving problems, developing new products, and deciding how to allocate their resources. The same tools have equivalent uses in nonprofits, education, and government. Those organizations need to create new products and services, to advertise effectively, and to solve various management problems. So, what exactly does that mean?

Creating Change has chapters devoted to brainstorming, to structured problem solving, to design, to strategic planning, to decision making, to problem analysis, and to collaborative strategies for innovation. You'll learn about pen-an-paper techniques and software. Most of the chapters end with lists of recommended books and web sites.

Chapter 2 invites readers to start creating a detailed strategy for integrating many innovation tools and techniques into their own social betterment efforts. A nine-part plan for social betterment innovation forms the meat of this chapter.

Chapter 3 builds on Chapter 2 by presenting a detailed justification for using a systematic approach to social innovation. This second chapter expands on the plan outlined in Chapter 2.

Chapters 4, 5, and 6 describe structured methods for evaluating problems and opportunities. Solving problems in existing social betterment efforts calls for logic, creativity, and structure in some cases. Chapter 3 presents many lists of questions that can help you explore a problem or opportunity in more detail. Chapter 4 presents a strategy for finding the cause of a problem, whether a management problem or a social problem. The technique is adapted from a management consulting technique usually applied to business problems. Chapter 5 presents tools for identifying potential problems and potential opportunities so that your organization is in a position to respond effectively.

Chapter 7 describes ideas you can steal and use to solve problems, sell ideas, and take better advantage of opportunities.

Brainstorming techniques are the subject of chapter 8. This chapter covers traditionally "creative" brainstorming techniques and some systematic ways of exploring a challenge for new ideas.

Chapter 9 builds on the subject of brainstorming by presenting an overview of brainstorming software. This software automates the creative techniques and the systematic ones, while often adding collaboration tools and evaluation to the idea generating processes.

A few enterprising business writers have created comprehensive strategies for creating and refining ideas. Chapter 10 presents two of these strategies and describes how to apply those strategies to social betterment efforts.

How do you know if your ideas are good ones? Chapter 11 focuses on this question, offering several tools for evaluating ideas.

Chapter 12 is all about decision making techniques. Decision-making isn't that tough, but sometimes a systematic approach is called for. The higher the stakes from a decision the more real data and systematic analysis need to be involved. This chapter covers several techniques for improving the quality of your decisions about programs, projects, allocation of resources, goals and objectives.

In Chapter 12 readers will learn how software can facilitate better problem solving, decision-making, and idea evaluation. Software also supports the all-important collaborative element of innovation. No, this chapter is not about using Google Drive and Slack to brainstorm. You'll instead learn about mind mapping software and other tools for analyzing problems and generating great ideas.

Chapters 13 describes several ways to organize creative problem solvers so that they can accomplish more

Ideas often have to be "sold" rather than implemented. Indeed this salesmanship is often the purpose of public education and social activism.

Chapter 14 describes some tools that can improve the marketability of your ideas.

Chapter 15 applies many of the tools and techniques to one of the author's own ideas for a nonprofit education and advocacy organization. Readers will learn how the material in *Creating Change* can be pulled together and used to create something real.

Creating Change ends with two appendices. Appendix 1 is a guide selecting the right tools and techniques to use for many common tasks. Appendix 2 lists and explains some useful concepts from business, psychology, and sociology. Use the descriptions and questions to help you apply the concepts to your own interests.

2 – A New System

Imagine this: A nonprofit dedicated to promoting sustainability in Nashville just started. The founders want to address many issues of conservation, waste, energy use, social inequality, and pollution. Of course they need to start somewhere. Of course they and their volunteer board hashed out a valid starting point. The charity will promote recycling an

Like most startup nonprofits, this one is being run on a shoestring budget. Founder One and Founder Two drew on some of their own savings and credit to get things going. They also managed to raise $1500 from friends and relatives. The founders recruited a few other folks to carry out some volunteer fundraising and advocacy work, to make up for not having the money to pay staff. Not a bad start all in all.

But, this imaginary organization faces many challenges. You can probably guess some of them based on your own life experience:

➤ Funding
➤ Breaking through the noise and clutter to get attention.
➤ Securing the money and in-kind contributions they need to grow
➤ Hiring and retaining qualified people
➤ Demonstrating their impact over time

Now, all of those challenges are common and all can be tackled in several ways. Usually, Founder One and Founder Two will have various tools they can use. They will have a book on fundraising tactics or a book on writing grant proposals.

This chapter offers a thorough introduction to this new social change system you read the outline of in Chapter 1. Not only will you learn what the system is, you'll learn why it makes a great deal of sense to adopt part of all of the system. Finally, you'll get a taste of how the system could work in an organization like yours, in dealing with challenges like yours.

Using a New System

A plan for weaving new brainstorming and problem-solving methods into the organization's work should be part of that strategic approach. Some questions need to be answered at the outset:

- Do you plan to work alone or involve other people?
- Which people should you "recruit"?
- What are your broad objectives – to sell an idea, to raise money, create an innovative public education campaign? Are you primarily concerned with problem solving, with getting new ideas, or with adopting existing ideas?
- How big do you need your problem solving efforts to be? How many people need to be involved? How many people do you intend to serve, educate, or influence? What is the geographic scope of your efforts?
- Are you starting a Web site, working with a community group, working in a nonprofit with national programs? How much money do you have?

The size of your organization will influence what you can accomplish in a given amount of time. The scale of the problem you want to address will also influence what you can expect to accomplish in a given amount of time. The scale of the problem may also influence your need for new ideas versus adaptation of original ideas. The complexity of a problem, and most social problems are complex, will influence your decision to focus on problem solving versus creative thinking about the problem. If you are starting a nonprofit, or want to start one, you may need both to analyze the issue that interests you and engage in some formal brainstorming to determine the best approach for your organization.

Advocacy efforts require creativity in crafting a message and reaching the appropriate people. Activists need to devise new demonstrations. Die-ins, people lying around pretending to be dead, used to be new and interesting. Maybe die-ins need to be replaced by something new, something that will better communicate the desired message to the desired audience. New strategies for effecting a certain change may be helpful, depending on the organization's resources and the results that the existing strategy is getting.

Conventional fundraising methods are fine, in the sense that they usually work reasonably well. What if you just want a new idea, one that might give better results for less effort? Maybe the organization needs to find a good fundraising strategy that will work without access to a grant writer or a big mailing list of potential donors. What if your board wants new and innovative fundraising ideas, but you don't have any? What if your organization is shut out of some common funding sources? New nonprofits often can't get grants. The lack of a track record can also be a deal-killer with business sponsors. Sure, you might possibly get a grant or a big sponsorship anyway, but the odds are slim and the investment of time can be significant.

Policies and programs often have room for improvement. Even if the policies don't need work they could probably be improved. Policies sometimes need to be "sold" to others who must vote on a policy or decide whether the policy will be implemented in an organization. Novel but practical policy designs might be valuable. Creative ways of selling the audience may also be needed. For businesses, an activist group may want to create a new policy that will achieve the activist group's goal while protecting the interests of management.

Programs for arts and culture nonprofits and for activist groups need to be designed or redesigned. The programs or the ways of marketing them can be improved in some way, perhaps. Brainstorming software can help people find ways to improve programs. Maybe the United States needs an alternative to the traditional financial management classes that are sometimes advertised to low-income people.

Social services organizations need to develop programs, administer programs, and improve programs. Maybe efficiency needs to be increased. Maybe the outcomes of a program, as measured by results, need to be improved. A high ratio of overhead to program costs, spending more than 25% of the organization's funds on overhead, for example, can look bad. The country's largest fundraising campaign, the Combined Federal Campaign, will reject an organization with operating costs are too high

Schools aren't very different from nonprofits when it comes to creating a strategy for integrating formal creativity methods and formal problem solving. You may want to use collaboration software if you work in a big school system, like the University of California. A school district may also need collaboration software. Brainstorming and problem solving meetings might be feasible. Schools and nonprofits also have budgets that probably won't support a large and expensive training effort. You may not be in a position to an expensive procurement effort started.

How many people do you want to be involved in this effort? You should probably start small. Recruit one or two people to study and practice brainstorming techniques, to use one example. Maybe you can start a bigger group. Maybe you can convince the big shots in your organization to invest in training or in enterprise software. Starting small is probably a better idea.

Determining the best starting place for your individual or group efforts is not too difficult. You only need to consider whether to go it alone or to involve other people. If you are striking out on your own then you have several options. You could begin rather simply, by reading a book on creativity or on problem solving. You could download trial brainstorming software and give it a try. The more ambitious sorts could start off by attending a class on lateral thinking, for example. Some training organizations do host classes that are open to the general public. More likely though, you would have to participate in company–sponsored training. The classes can be hard to find and can be rather expensive, over $1500.

The next steps are easy enough: buy more software, recruit someone to work with you, get someone to come to your organization and teach a class. The Resources section of this chapter lists places you can go for more information on trainers and software.

But, do you really need to form a group or can you work alone? If you are responsible for bringing ideas to the group or solving a problem then the answer is simple: take the initiative to learn something and use it. Most of us actually work with others on solving problems, implementing new ideas, or starting an organization. If that describes your situation, you could still stick with doing things on your own. Or you could recruit someone else to work with you. Ask someone to read the same book you read and discuss how to apply the techniques. Encourage a computer-loving partner to try the brainstorming software you've been experimenting with.

If you are willing and able to start a group the first question to ask is whether you can meet physically or if virtual meetings make better sense. In most cases it will make better sense to meet in person. Given that the world is becoming more connected and activists can collaborate with people across the globe, there are times when some form of "virtual brainstorming" makes the most sense.

Go beyond doing a simple SWOT analysis. It won't take much extra time. Read on to find out how your normal strategic planning activities can be opportunities for new thinking.

Challenges and Opportunities

The world is full of both problems to solve and opportunities to exploit. Entrepreneurs, managers, and executives are keenly aware of those facts. Likewise, many people in the social sector are familiar with the practice of looking for problems and opportunities real or potentially real. That's not the issue here.

Explore the social environment for current opportunities and for potential future opportunities is important. Being aware of real or potential problems is also important. Sure, problems usually become apparent at some point because they are problems. The symptoms present themselves and we decide to take action. Maybe our response is good enough to solve the problem and maybe not. It would almost always be more effective to see the problem coming and take steps to prevent it or to develop a coping strategy. Can we prevent global climate change or merely adapt to the effects?

Some problems really can't be solved, at least by you or by your organization. A workaround of some sort needs to be devised. A nonprofit that uses a raffle as its principle fundraising tool may find that raffles are going to be illegal soon. The organization can't expect to stop that legislation; the only solution is to find a new source of revenue. Substance abuse can't be stopped, but we can come up with better ways to discourage substance abuse or to mitigate the impacts on peoples' lives. Maybe there are some unrealized opportunities in mitigating the impacts of substance abuse on your community?

Some opportunities are obvious and important. Opportunities that aren't so obvious may be quite valuable anyway. Finding opportunities to raise more money, serve more people, get better results, or gain media attention for issues are always welcome. Some opportunities or potential future opportunities are going to come to our attention in the normal course of our work. Others will only appear if we can spare a little time each week to look for them. Potential threats/challenges/problems will be easier to see and deflect by setting aside time to scan for them.

Strategic Thinking Strategies

Any strategy has to have a focus and any strategic planning process needs a structure. What do you want to achieve? How, in general, do you want to achieve that goal? What process will you use? What interim objectives do you want/need to reach? Does your objective relate to changing behaviors, educating people, recruiting volunteers, or changing something specific in the law? Answering such questions should be the beginning of any strategic approach to innovation in the social sector. Those are a few of the possibilities. You need to decide if your real aim is public education, a specific social change such as outlawing abortion, raising more money, getting more people to enroll in a government-sponsored program, or something else entirely. Once you've got that answer it will be easier to know whether you should focus on learning creative thinking techniques or problem analysis or decision analysis, or design thinking. In any case, you'll benefit greatly if you can learn and use one new technique in each of those areas.

Several possible processes could be helpful. There are general techniques of brainstorming, systematic idea generation (logical forms of brainstorming), problem analysis, and decision analysis. There are also comprehensive approaches to innovation. Engineers have TRIZ (theory of inventive problem solving). Nonprofits have lateral thinking®, design thinking, Einstein thinking, and other comprehensive procedures for getting workable new ideas.

Your strategic goal could be to educate the public so that some critical mass of people recognizes X as a problem. People will start to demand that corporate executives or government officials do something about X. Maybe there is a political gap to be filled. We need a law or regulation or policy. You can't track current events for more than a few days before you encounter some person or group who wants a particular law, policy, or regulation.

You may want to start building a strategy by scanning the environment. All groups and formal organizations operate in a social environment consisting of people, laws, regulations, economic conditions, technologies, cultural values, and natural resources to name a few elements of the social environment. You may want to institute a formal scanning process to check out the social environment. Systematically assessing the strengths of your organization, its weaknesses, threats from the social environment, and opportunities in the social environment constitutes the dominant process of scanning the environment.

SWOT (strengths, weaknesses, opportunities, and threats)

analysis, as it is called in strategic planning literature, is standard practice and can be learned without too much difficulty. Many organizations rely on facilitated strategic planning workshops because this ensures that professionals are leading the analysis. Those workshops aren't cheap. Small community groups and nonprofit organizations who want to do any environmental scanning or strategic planning will need to substitute time for money. Check the end of this chapter for resources on strategic planning and environmental scanning.

Studying the social environment needs to be a regular activity and not something that happens when you decide to update your strategic plan. The best method for content analysis is to read things, lots of things. Read to find information on politics, economic trends, and popular culture. Real and proposed legislation of certain types may also be relevant. New social science research, particularly in various branches of psychology can also be valuable. Your primary sources should be scholarly journals, specialized Web sites, and specialty magazines. Anything published in a news magazine or book is probably old news to experts. Popular magazines that touch on subjects like sociology, psychology, and environmental issues may be more timely in the news they report.

Where do you steal ideas from anyway? Well, content analysis may help. You will see a program or policy or education strategy that's working in a different context. Maybe the education idea was created for high school students. Is there anything to stop you from stealing the idea and using it to educate adults in the community? Nope. Ideas can't be patented or copyrighted. Books and magazines from outside your area of work and outside your personal sphere of interests may also be useful. Maybe you can get a good idea from a magazine on World War

II history or a book on goal setting.

Do you need a new idea and not just one that's already been used elsewhere? Content analysis can show you a new idea that you can use. The idea still needs to be adapted to your particular circumstances. This process may be relatively straightforward. Or, you may need to create a slightly different "design" for your borrowed idea. And completely different ideas can also be useful if you apply some imagination. Asking outrageous questions can help. How can a vending machine get inner city poor people more interested in their health? You'll learn a method for answering that question in Chapter 2.

Stealing Ideas

Consider design thinking. As Edward De Bono points out the cause of a problem can be something that cannot be remedied or removed, at least by any imaginable human effort. If "human nature" is at the root of the problem, or seems to be a major contributor then you have to create a new way to move forward. You leave human nature alone and find a way to work around it.

Wide-ranging reading interests form the foundation for good idea stealing. How else will you find something to steal? Well, wide-ranging Web surfing and conversation work too. In fact, all three approaches should be part of an effort to find ideas that can be copied, adapted, or combined in some way. Reading about a variety of subjects will naturally expose you to new concepts and innovations that might be helpful in some way. Conversations will people working in different fields or in the same field can lead to new ideas and insights.

Where to Find New Ideas

Ideas can come from anywhere, but some sources are going to be better than others. Articles, blogs, and books that could furnish good ideas aren't always obvious. You might find inspiration or useful advice in writing on subjects only distantly related to whatever your nonprofit's mission is, or whatever the challenge is.

Look for books, magazine articles, and Web content that covers the subjects in each list. You might also want to sign up for classes and take ideas from what you learn there. A class on writing for the Web could obviously teach you how to make an online marketing effort more effective. The appendix to this book offers some specific suggestions too. Advocacy requires "selling" one or more ideas so anything in the areas of marketing or branding or the psychology of persuasion could help.

Don't stick with literature that's directly related to whatever you do. Creative problem solving often leads people far afield of where they normally work. A magazine devoted to classic cars might lead to a new idea for promoting recycling. A parenting magazine might contain a glossy ad that suggests a new way to fund an adult literacy program. Make it a point to sometimes read stuff that's completely out of your field and look for ideas.

Design Thinking

Our culture, including values, norms, beliefs, and technology, may be missing something that's relevant to solving a problem or exploiting an opportunity. Problem analysis is likely to be needed here, so you can identify what needs to be created, changed or improved.

Specific processes and concepts that support design thinking can be learned and used by anyone. Design of social innovations is not some esoteric craft that only the university educated can master. Considering the fit between your idea and the community or organization that's supposed to use the idea is not difficult to do. The point is to consider the value, fit and other elements in a systematic fashion.

What about the "gaps" in society between how things do work and could work? Those gaps are places where new ideas need to be created and sold. Maybe there are problems that have gone unsolved because no solution that will sell has yet been put forth. Maybe the problem has not, as yet, been recognized as a problem. Maybe you can see an opportunity to improve society in some way. There is no real problem, just a way to do more of something or to do something better. You can probably think of something about society that is not an actual problem but could be made better. Go ahead and think of something, then start reading again.

Creative Thinking

New ideas, variations on existing ideas, and novel combinations of ideas might be needed. Any sort of social betterment effort is likely to need new ideas from time-to-time. New ideas can mean better fundraising results, more people changing a certain behavior, or an idea that becomes a ballot initiative. There are books, card decks (yes, card decks), classes, and software available.

Starting off with one or two simple techniques applied with the help of a pen and a piece of paper might just do the trick. If not, there are sophisticated techniques that may give better results. Some creative-thinking techniques are intuitive – they are probably the sorts of tools you would think of when you think of brainstorming – but logical techniques also exist.

Creativity can be a solitary effort, but probably shouldn't be! Involve other people to generate ideas, evaluate ideas, or to refine your thinking about what counts as a good idea. Collaboration doesn't even require being in the same area as the other people. The Internet makes it easy to work together on brainstorming, evaluating ideas, improving ideas, and implementing ideas.

Software can help whether you go it alone or work with a group to generate and refine ideas. There is specialized software to facilitate solo brainstorming, group brainstorming, and major efforts to innovate. Brainstorming software can cost anywhere from $0 to thousands. Some of the software is quite simple to use, like a text-editing program, while other titles are more like professional desktop publishing packages.

Knowledge gaps can be a problem when we need to vote on a ballot initiative, on a politician, or make a significant purchase decision. Do people know what social scientists consider the main contributors to crime, or overuse of credit? If not, maybe their votes or their political activism will not give desirable results. Creative thinking can help us find ways of closing that knowledge gap through innovative advertising efforts. Maybe creating lessons for colleges or secondary schools would work. Information gathering can tell us where the knowledge gap exists and how big it is and even what some of the consequences are.

Decision analysis can help us to choose a good way of addressing the knowledge gap. We can see the likely consequences of a certain decision's implementation. We can also systematically and with reduced bias see the pros and cons of a course of action. We can make better-informed decisions by leaning to prioritize ideas according to an explicit set of criteria.

Scientific Thinking

The desire to make things happen and feel like we are doing something important really shouldn't get in the way of facts, logic, and theory. Facts are obviously important to understanding an issue. But they also help us determine if our program or project is really working and how well. Focusing on the facts keeps us grounded in reality. How many well-intentioned efforts have fallen short because the relevant facts got ignored? How much money and effort were wasted?

Logic forces us to make arguments that hold together when we examine the premises and assumptions behind our ideas. We can also apply some logic to other peoples' ideas. For activists, this is a good tactic to use in fighting someone else's opposing idea. Logic can lead to insights that change peoples' perceptions of an issue, policy, program, attitude, or behavior.

Theories are not guesses. Theories are descriptions of the ways in which groups of phenomena are related. The theory of evolution is a set of propositions that explain many changes in living things over billions of years. A theory of deviance can help us identify ways of combating juvenile delinquency. Selling an idea based on science rather than an ideologically based opinion about what ought to be done is a separate issue. Good luck!

Social science research can help us understand an issue and can lend credibility to our cause. Of course, that credibility only goes so far, since ideology and emotion tend to trump facts. The research also helps us understand the mechanisms that lead to social conditions that we want to change.

Science is based on facts, logic, and descriptions of relationships between phenomena that can be observed. What does this mean for your innovation or social change efforts? How do scientific thinking, creative problem solving, problem analysis, decision analysis, idea evaluation, and the selling of an idea fit together? Facts are "selling points" for an idea. Statistics, both good and bad, may support your idea and its value. Has substance abuse among teens been on the rise in your community? Don't just tell us that it is so. Give us some numbers and the credible source they came from. Use facts to help you understand the source of a problem. Again, statistics that relate to the scale or nature of a problem can be helpful.

Developing and testing hypotheses about a problem can be even more helpful. Hypothesis testing sounds like an esoteric intellectual exercise, but it can actually be quite simple. You'll learn more about forming hypotheses, testing them, and using the results in Chapter 4.

Logic can help you make a case for something. This much is obvious. But you also need to use logic on your own plans and ideas. You need to think objectively about your cause; objectivity is another trait associated with scientists. Scientists have opinions and beliefs but those things are usually suppressed in favor of a value-neutral examination of the subject under study. Activists may object to objectivity. We know domestic violence is a big problem. We know domestic violence has to be stopped. How can anyone approach the fight against domestic violence in a coldly rational way, like a machine?

Pure rationality is not the point, and can't be achieved anyway. The point is to try and divorce thinking about what ought to be done, which is rightly the domain of human values, with how things ought to be done, which should be largely objective. Of course values still have

a role to play in guiding our selection of strategies and tactics.

Logic can spare us from pursuing silly ideas that we can't sell

to anyone and that may not do any good even if they are implemented.

Consider the errors in logic listed in this list:

- Ambiguous terms
- Unidentified information sources
- Invalid generalizations
- Reliance on analogies
- Selected, supportive information
- Appeals to authority
- Red herrings(unrelated issues, tangents)
- Mudslinging (attacking the other side)
- Emotionally loaded terms, arguments
- Slippery slope arguments

Could you get yourself or other people in trouble if you're

thinking is tainted by one of those logical fallacies? Probably. Your

credibility with a skeptical and potentially hostile public or government

is on the line. You wouldn't support a plan that rests mainly on the idea

that Congress is full of pinhead conservatives would you? Would you?

You can't expect the conservative or moderate public to take seriously

such weak thinking. It will seem obvious that we are being manipulated.

Appeals to emotion can be effective, or they can backfire horribly.

Claiming that the terrorists could blow up New York City one day,

might alienate rather than motivate so try to avoid hyperbole.

Aside from the strength or weakness of our own logic,

knowing the rules can help us fight the other side(s) in a debate. Are they saying a proposal will start an inevitable slide into barbarism? Did they accuse someone on your side of being a crazy communist? Use those two sins against clear thought to show us why we can't trust the other guy. Start keeping a written record of logical fallacies that are being arrayed against your cause.

Numbers are important to any effort at changing society or improving peoples' lives. The right data will tell you where you are, whether things are getting better or worse and whether your efforts are paying off or not. Finding and understanding statistical data is not hard, really. Using the data to help you understand or publicize the issue in question is also not that hard. True, social scientists do use sophisticated techniques to model behavior and describe relationships between social phenomena. You don't need to know much, if anything, about those methods. Some information on those advanced statistical topics can be found in the Recommended Reading section at the end of this chapter.

Many books and Web sites combine to offer a flood of statistics that might help you. It can be a bit like opening your over-full closet and having things spill out closet all over the floor. You can manage this problem by starting with a few tried and true sources. The United States Census Bureau conducts several surveys, including the famous decennial census. Those surveys are an incredibly rich source of economic and demographic data offered at varying levels of geographic detail. The U.S. Bureau of Labor Statistics also publishes extensive data on business and employment. The Environmental Protection agency may have useful statistics on environmental quality. The Department of Justice may be able to furnish statistics on criminal behavior. State governments will generally the same sorts of data available at the state level. Some city governments will also have

As you consider what data you need and how you will use it, there are a couple of often-violated rules you should keep in mind. Rates and percentages are typically more important than raw numbers. Trends are also more important than raw numbers in many cases. What percent of teenagers in your city were arrested between 2010 and 2019? Is the percentage increasing or decreasing? An organization that wants to fight juvenile delinquency by giving teenagers positive things to work for could benefit from asking questions about the rates of different behaviors. That information can help them decide how to focus their energies.

Statistics have at least four general uses. The right data can help people decide how to focus their resources. Statistics can be good public education tools. Numbers are a convenient way to show the scale of the problem or a trend, positive or negative. Statistics could also help an organization raise money through grants or fundraising letters or appeals on Web sites. Finally, statistics can help in attempts to change behavior. A university could fight binge drinking on campus by reporting data on what percentage of students say they never have more than five drinks when they drink.

Analytical Thinking

Study the parts of a challenge and see how they relate to one another. Look for influences from the political environment, the natural environment, technology, demographics, or the local economy. No problem or opportunity exists in a vacuum, as you well know. The point is to take that common sense idea and apply it as needed.

Instead of asserting that the root of the problem is X or Y, state a specific hypothesis about the problem. Identify evidence that would show whether the hypothesis is true or false. Then, analyze the evidence and act on the results. That process is similar to, but less rigorous than, the standard scientific process.

Ask questions about your challenge. Explore the likely root of the problem, the contributing factors that can make things worse (or better!), and the criteria that a solution has to meet. Ask questions about the characteristics of a good solution to a challenge.

Analytical thinking will not replace emotion or ideology. That would be unrealistic and undesirable, at least in the case of replacing emotion with cold calculation. Analytical thinking is more relevant to the arguable useful task of forming a buffer between our emotions and biases and the decision to engage in a particular action.

Marketing Mindset

Activists, fundraisers, and anyone with an education message or program to promote are participating in a marketplace. Programs, policies, and behavior changes have to be sold to the appropriate audience. Why should someone donate to your cause instead of another, or instead of just keeping their money? Activists must compete for attention and money with other causes, peoples' hobbies, and commercial products and services. It can't hurt to consider the audience for your message or idea:

1. Who is the audience?
2. How can you reach them?
3. What do they want? What do they care about?
4. How do they think about the world?

5. What benefits can you offer your audience?

6. What evidence can you present to show that your audience will get the benefits?

7. What exactly do you want your audience to do?

All nine elements of systematic social innovation work for any sort of social betterment effort. Social activism obviously calls for some strategic thinking and applied imagination. Education, whether through schools or public education campaigns, calls for scientific thinking and a willingness to steal ideas. Fundraising efforts often need a little creativity and a strategic focus. Program and policy development calls for analytical thinking, scientific thinking, and creativity. Activism, program design, policy development, and public education often call for some good marketing.

Social Innovation Strategy

Changing something in the structure of society – including the relationships between different groups of people – may be your strategic focus. You'll need some tools for determining which structural gap your group should focus on. Then you'll need to create or adapt ideas. You may need to do some problem analysis first. What is the cause of this problem in the structure of society? How do we act to improve things? Creative thinking can help you identify options. Having specific rules for judging ideas will help you pick a good idea. Creative thinking can help you sell your idea to citizens, corporate executives, or politicians.

Of course you have to implement a strategy for it to do any good. You need to have tactics that you can use, and then you have to use those tactics. How do you develop tactics that will support your strategy? We come back to the issue of creativity. You may have standard tactics you can use in, for example, demonstrations against something. You may find tactics from other fields that would work. Brainstorming using one or more formal techniques may produce workable new tactics.

How do you implement a strategy? In part, this question was answered earlier in the chapter. You have to decide whether to buy a book, take a class, download free software, or talk to coworkers about what to do. Try to learn the software or techniques you read about in a book by working on a real challenge. Why wait to start attacking a problem or trying to exploit an opportunity. OK, so identifying the cause(s) of a problem may be the right first step. The right first step may also be to look at approaches to an opportunity that you've discovered. How can you best proceed and take advantage of the opportunity? What is your first move? What is your second move?

Where will you implement your strategic approach? If you head a nonprofit, then the answer is obvious. Or maybe the answer isn't so obvious. Maybe management staff only needs to be involved. Maybe some program staff and volunteers need to be involved. What will you do first? Telling everyone to read a particular book is a good start. You could get some used copies online for a reasonable amount of money. I've seen used creative-thinking books for under $5 on Amazon.com

Do you need to get professional help? What sort of help do you need? There are three possibilities to consider. You could hire a consultant to walk your group through a problem-solving exercise or a strategic planning session. This is certainly a reasonable approach. The second option you have is to call in a trainer to teach lateral thinking, problem analysis, or other tools and techniques. You may need an

outside consultant to install and configure software. Some collaborative
software is quite complex. The third option involves consultants but
may not be so obvious: hire a consultant to help you reproduce a
program/service/solution that's being used somewhere else. You could
figure out to copy almost anything on your own. Hiring an expert will
save time and money and probably considerable frustration.

3 – Solving the Right Problem

Everyone knows about brainstorming. Most of us have done some informal brainstorming. Maybe the results were useful and maybe not. Some people have learned formal techniques for generating new ideas. This chapter describes some of those techniques and the two options for using the techniques: pen-and-paper, or computer software. Individual and group techniques exist. You should know something about each sort of brainstorming. After all, most of us work with other people sometimes. Software can only be described in a general way since products and manufacturers come and go. I will mention some titles that have been around for a few years and seem to come from stable companies.

Problem solving in general is another process we are all familiar with. Just as there are formal techniques for brainstorming, there are many formal techniques for problem solving. Activists need to have one or two of those problem solving tools at their disposal.

Understanding the Problem

Much of what goes before can also apply to problem-solving methods. Your informal analysis of a problem may be adequate, or not. Often social problems and problems in organization's have multiple causes. By definition, the cause of a problem is not known. A problem is any deviation from the desired performance, where the cause of the deviation is unknown as defined in *The New Rational Manager*. A formal approach offers more structure. Relevant facts, relationships, and hypotheses are more likely to get attention. Our own biases and perceptions will tend to color an informal analysis of the problem. This coloring effect is likely to be especially acute in advocacy or social activism. We have decided that we know what to do. We need to ban this or regulate that, or stop people from doing something. When we have "discovered" the source of the problem we tend to go right to a specific solution, specific strategies, and specific tactics. This is not a bad thing really. We depend on being able to find standardized or routine responses to the problems we encounter. Edward De Bono made that point in *New Thinking for the New Millennium.*

In creating new social institutions, programs, policies, and education initiatives we have the additional problem of emotions and ideological biases. We see the solution in our own emotional reactions, reaching for one certain solution that occurs to us. Or, we find a solution in a certain ideological perspective. The radical leftist finds a leftist solution and starts to work. Sometimes people do good things when they go on emotional and/or ideological crusades. One woman got dozens of nations to stop using land mines. Adam Walsh, whose son was kidnapped and beheaded in the 1980s, founded the highly successful Center for Missing and Exploited Children.

Still, the general point about structuring your analysis of an issue stands. The techniques you will learn about in Chapter 4 will help structure the problem solving process. Use the techniques and you will be able to make better decisions about how to proceed. Studying the factors contributing to a social or environmental problem can only improve your solution. At the very least, you will have a better chance of selling one of your ideas if you can present supporting facts.

Knowing What to Do

These thoughts about creativity and problem analysis are all interesting, but we already know what needs to be done. You may have had that thought while reading, maybe even before that. You would naturally know what to do after being involved in an issue or cause for some time. But do you know the best, *practical* thing you can do to change peoples' minds, design a better policy, or create a better social program? What if someone challenged you to come up with a way to do more with your budget or create better results for clients with no more money or staff? Do you know how to analyze an idea for weaknesses? Is there some opportunity that you have overlooked?

Taking a formal approach to creativity and a structured approach to problem solving is the way to cope with those kinds of questions. When you know a reliable way to generate ideas, evaluate them, and strengthen them you will never go for long without a workable new idea. A shortage of money or staff becomes both a creative challenge and a way to sell your bold new idea: "I have this idea for streamlining our work so we can handle 30 extra cases without another staff person." A structured problem solving approach may lead to different conclusions about a problem. Is your novel approach to teen drug abuse really addressing the source of the problem?

Many political proposals address nothing in particular. They are created so government officials can say they are doing something about an issue that citizens are complaining about. Companies are not much better in this regard. They pretend to be "green" or "socially responsible" and create advertising campaigns to tell us they care. Governments create ideologically driven policies and programs that are sometimes created without any reference to facts or analysis. The way to deal with crime is to build more jails and hire more cops. The reasoning here is probably that people choose to become criminals and so we need to deter people from being bad or lock them up. "Scared straight" programs in schools appeal to conservatives despite any evidence that they do work or could work. Most people don't carefully consider the consequences of criminal behavior until the act has been committed.

Pen and paper work perfectly well so why bother with software. Some of it costs serious money and might be hard to use. Why pay for software? What sort of software should you use? Well, if you are interested solely in brainstorming new ideas, there is reasonably cheap mind mapping software. Mind mapping is a brainstorming technique that you'll learn more about in Chapter 8. Using software that works in a variety of situations and helps you evaluate your ideas is also a good idea. You can get this type of comprehensive software for under $200 a copy. Software that allows people to collaborate online, and that is made just for generating ideas, would cost more. A geographically dispersed organization may want to make the investment anyway.

Why pay for mind mapping software in particular? Can't people just draw their maps? If you are the only one who needs to see or use the mindmap then using pen and paper is no problem. However, software can produce neat and attractive mind maps that are easily exported to presentation software or word processing software. Complex diagrams are almost impossible to create with presentation software or word processing software. Diagramming software like Microsoft Visual Studio is a little too complicated and expensive for simple mind mapping. Some mind mapping software can cost over $200 but some versions are considerable less than $100. FreeMind is a free, open-source tool for mind mapping.

The first question that crosses many peoples' minds is this: Why do we need to use a formal technique or techniques to brainstorm new ideas? Some people will wonder how much creativity is really called for if plenty of ideas already exist. The truth is that hoping for the right idea to present itself is not a good strategy. Hope is not a strategy, as the title of one popular business book advised us. The quality and quantity of ideas that come from informal brainstorming may not be good. You may not have carefully defined what counts as a good idea. That too is part of formal brainstorming. You should spell out the characteristics that a good idea must possess.

Good Ideas

Good ideas have several characteristics in common. Like good goals, good ideas need to be realistic. A good idea needs to be logically linked to the desired result. Science and logic will help determine whether an idea really fits the goal. Good ideas are realistic given the time and other resources that are available.

The relationship between the mechanism that contributes to a problem and your idea needs to be supported by evidence. Why will banning handgun ownership in the United States reduce murder rates? This question might seem easy to answer, but don't be so quick about saying so. Reading scholarly research on the effects of gun control might not turn up a clear connection between murder rates and handgun ownership rates. Assuming there is a connection between handgun ownership and murder rates our campaign against handgun ownership makes some sense. Other factors might actually have a bigger impact on murder rates than access to handguns, so we can only say that the idea of banning handguns makes *some* sense. Other approaches may be more effective and/or efficient ways of reducing the murder rate.

Deciding Where to Start

So, cost should not be a huge barrier to using innovation tools in your group or organization. Software is usually not too expensive. Getting a book of two from the library is free. Or, you can get just the titles you want from a large online bookstore and spend less than $10 a copy. Training and consulting are much more expensive, of course. Idea management software – you use it for managing idea generation over an Intranet or the Web – is expensive. What you pay for is obviously going to depend on a your interest level in innovation, your resources, and your tolerance for risk. Rolling out a big idea management system will be expensive in money and staff time and could be a flop. Or, it could be a huge success. Buying books for yourself and your staff, with the intent of applying the methods described, would be much cheaper. Your chances of at least a modest success are also quite high.

Should you do things yourself or get professional help? Well, you have to know yourself and your staff and coworkers. If everyone in the group is a self-directed learner, then reading a book or two is a good starting point. Buying software and figuring it out is also a viable option. Just keep in mind that no training of any sort is available for most creativity software. On the other hand, most of the software is relatively easy to use.

Learning complicated brainstorming techniques or solving a

difficult problem may be something you are confident of handling on your own. Or, you may decide to hire someone. Some training classes are open to the public and not just put on for specific clients. Assuming you can afford the fee, the classes are a good option. Most people learn better in a structured environment. The classes also tend to come with travel and lodging costs since you aren't likely to find one that's being held nearby at a convenient time.

Using all of these tools and learning to use them is also a significant investment of time. So, as with cost, you need to weigh how much you need to accomplish against the significant time investment. You can start off cheaply, and you can start off with a low investment of time and energy. Get involved in things that are more time consuming as your schedule allows or as your innovation needs demand more powerful and complex tools. Learning the techniques described in *The Activism Book* should only take a few hours of reading and practicing.

Business Ideas

One of the key components of creative problem solving is the ability to find and adapt ideas that are being used successfully in other areas. The business world offers a great source of ideas for nonprofits, governments, schools, and social entrepreneurs. Businesses have products and services to sell. Businesses try to position themselves in customers' minds as the best solution for some problem that consumers have. Businesses obviously engage in marketing efforts of all sorts. Businesses are always looking for new products, services, products, and marketing tricks. Would-be social changers could learn a few tricks from the business world. The trick is to know how to find ideas and how to adapt them to the social sector.

Consider some common marketing tricks that businesses use. Maybe those methods will spark ideas. Maybe something from the list that follows will spark an idea you can use. Of course you'll start out by defining a problem or opportunity that you'd like to tackle.

1. Coupons
2. Midnight madness sales
3. Clearance sales
4. Special events, like fashion shows and celebrity autograph sessions
5. Sponsorships, especially of sports teams

Figure out what counts as a good idea for your particular circumstances, and then think about a business practice to borrow. Defining a focus for your efforts, evaluating the possibilities and deciding what to do are all necessary steps in a serious innovation effort. Chapters 3, 8, and 11 offer more guidance on doing those things.

The Marketing Mindset

You will probably not be able to accomplish much on your own. Changing society, improving the community, and starting a new project in an organization all take some degree of salesmanship. Nowhere is this truer than in social marketing: getting people to change their own behavior for their own benefit (as opposed to promoting behavior change to sell more stuff) self-help books). Thinking like a marketer means keeping a couple of things in mind.

The most important element of thinking like a marketer is to remember that you are selling something. You are selling the idea that people need to vote a certain way, adopt a certain behavior, think a certain way, or stop a behavior. It can only help your case if you can appeal to peoples' interests. You could tap into one of the things that motivate people. Psychologists identify and classify desires in different ways, including the motivators in this list:

- Acceptance
- Acknowledgment
- Contribution
- Consistency
- Family
- Novelty
- Physical Security
- Power

How could you use one or more of those motivators in an advertisement, editorial, letter to the editor, essay, Web page or speech? You could even try tapping into one or two motivators with a sign or banner or small newspaper ad.

Appeal to peoples' interests/needs/wants. People are always reading an advertising message and wondering what's in it for them. What's the benefit for me if I swear off meat? What do I get out of going to all of the trouble to find locally grown organic produce? If you don't know, then you don't have a viable social marketing effort.

In *Jump Start Your Business Brain*, Doug Hall presents two more ideas that could be transferred to the world of social change. What is the real reason to believe that if I do what you want I will get the benefits you claim? Marketers also use a unique selling proposition

(USP), a benefit that consumers can only get from that product or service. What benefit can your program, service, or idea give people that they can't get, at least in equal measure anywhere else?

Online Innovation Resources

The internet is an indispensable resource for activists and others who want to create and sell new ideas. Many Web sites offer tips or instructions covering all phases of brainstorming and problem solving. Mindtools.com offers free information on brainstorming tools and decision-making techniques. Online bookstores offer access to more creativity, innovation, decision making, and problem solving books than you could ever hope to find at a library or a brick-and-mortar bookstore.

Web sites also offer ideas you can use, at least for inspiration. The best of these sites is undoubtedly the Global Idea Bank, where you can find thousands of social innovations described in varying levels of detail. The site also offers books of social innovations. You can even submit your own ideas and possibly win the site's annual £1,000 prize for the year's best social innovation. Worldchanging.com, companion site to the bestseller *Worldchanging: A User's Guide to the 21st Century*, offers tons of information on new technologies and ideas. If neither site happens to be helpful, try a Google search for "social innovations."

Many sites devoted to social innovation, either promoting it or funding it, have popped up. The crowdfunding site Kickstarter is probably the most famous example of a place you can go to raise money for a new program or project. Kickstarter focuses on business ideas, but nonprofits still have a chance there. Other crowdfunding sites

exist, and will likely come and go over the years. As of late 2012,
Kickstarter and Indiegogo are the big players. Indiegogo is the place to
go with a   nonprofit project or program to promote.

Not sure how to start or run a crowdfunding effort? If you aren't
even sure that this crowdfunding thing makes sense for your
organization, Kickstarter and Indiegogo offer advice on how to run a
good campaign. Nonprofit resources like *Nonprofit Times*, the *Stanford
Social Innovation Review*, and the *Chronicle of Philanthropy* cover
social innovation, crowdfunding, design thinking, creativity, and
related topics. Add one or two of those resources to your reading list if
they aren't there now.

Stealing ideas and working with concepts are two important
elements of creativity, and tw3o things that Web sites are certainly
good for. Look for ideas to steal at one of those innovation sites. Hunt
for concepts to steal on sites devoted to sociology and psychology. A
"concept" is a general way of doing something. Exaggerating a
problem is a concept one could use to get people to change their
behavior.

The Web might lead you to research that you can use. For
example, if you understand your audience and their social environment
you have a much better idea of successfully implementing a new idea.
Statistics and trends are good to know for many reasons. At a minimum,
a statistic from a reputable source can add credibility to a fundraising
appeal. Social science research can also suggest a new project or
program, or even a new approach to dealing with a social problem.

Training and Consulting:

Innovation and problem solving can both be quite complex. The more factors to consider the harder it can be to do the right thing. The higher the stakes in a given situation, the more important it is to proceed carefully. While most techniques you might need are amenable to self-directed learning, formal training may be in order. Many people, perhaps most people, aren't much good at self-teaching unless they happen to be fascinated by a subject. So, taking classes in Lateral Thinking® or Internet research may make sense. Read on and you'll see the value of Internet research.

Consultants are already experts at dealing with certain sorts of issues or in applying certain methodologies. Assuming a consultant's fees fit the budget, it might make sense to get some professional help. A consultant could expertly run a group brainstorming session, or help you develop a new strategy. The Resources section at the end of this chapter lists places to find consultants.

Results, or Possible Results

What can you really expect to get out of using the brainstorming, problem analysis, and decision making tools? That's a fair question, so here are some examples:

1. A fundraising campaign could raise significantly more money.
2. A government employment agency could place more people in jobs in less time.
3. A public education effort intended to keep middle-school students from smoking could get more kids to abstain.
4. A school could cut the number of fights (fistfights and shouting matches) by 90%, or more. Edward De Bono reports that fights in a South African mine were cut by 98% after miners learned

some "thinking tools" developed by De Bono.

5. An activist group could get more minutes, or column inches of press coverage, which translates to more attention to the group's idea.

4 – Asking Good Questions

Questions are the basis of any good social innovation or creative activism effort. This chapter is about exploring your social environment, examining your assumptions, and thinking about your problem or challenge. We need to ask ourselves questions about all those things. What counts as a good idea? What resources do we have? What resources do we need to acquire and how would we acquire them? Is this a problem or a symptom of a deeper problem? What is changing in our social environment? What do these changes mean in terms of potential problems and opportunities?

Management gurus have invented many sets of questions that organize your exploration of a challenge. These questions support planning, analysis, idea generation, and decision making. The Five Why technique for exploring the root of a problem, and to explore your motivations, is covered later in this chapter. Charles W. McCoy lists many such questions in his book *Why Didn't I Think of That? Think the Unthinkable and Achieve Creative Greatness*. The following four sections list some of the questions and some comments on their use in social betterment. Many questions uniquely designed for the social sector are also offered here.

Questions About Your Environment

1. How many non-profits operate in the area? How many have a similar mission and/or program?

2. How quickly is the environment changing and in what ways? Think of environmental quality, cultural, demographics, legal, economic, everything that might present a problem or provide an opportunity.)

3. How many natural resources are there that we could use? (Yes, thinking about open space, land, and water can be useful even if your organization isn't concerned with environmental issues – where would you hold events? What orgs or volunteer groups do environmental work and is there a way pool your resources? Think about it.)

4. How many sources of financial support can we identify? (Consider all sorts of grants and local businesses that supported causes like yours in the past.)

5. How quickly is the local economy changing, and in what ways?

6. How much financial support is available for non-profit organizations? (This is about the pool of money and in-kind contributions not the number of places you could go.)

7. How many different groups of people are there, and where do they live? (Thinking of interest groups, religious groups, ethnic groups, out-of-state college students could be helpful.)

8. What is the rate of change in the population we serve? (Population growth, overall or in one demographic can be an opportunity or a challenge in several ways.)

9. How big is the pool of likely consumers (of our services) What about donors?

10. How many laws and regulations are relevant to our work, clients, or audience? (This question is to check that you understand the complete "legal landscape" that's relevant to your mission.)

11. How many changes are there in the "legal landscape" described by those questions? (In other words, what definite changes or potential changes like new regulations or new legislation is coming along?)

12. What could laws and regulations allow us to do, that we aren't doing now?

13. How many competing, and collaborating interest groups are there? (Consider volunteer groups, Meetups, online groups, groups that meet in real life, and so on.)

14. How much is the political climate changing, and in how many ways? (Are there any real or probable changes in the local or state government that would present a challenge or an opportunity.)

15. What is the political climate for change? (Are things becoming more liberal or conservative? Is the government turning thriftier or is it looking to spend more on "social betterment" projects?)

16. How many technological options are there? (This question is about the kinds of technologies you might use to raise money, educate, advocate, streamline your operations and so on. Think beyond information technology to include processes, hardware, physical tools, vehicles, et cetera.)

17. What new technologies should we be looking at now? (This question is about emerging technologies that might be helpful?)

18. How are those technologies changing? (Look for what's becoming more common, what is fading in popularity, getting less expensive or more user-friendly.)

19. How many different cultures and subcultures are relevant to your organization? (This is a question about local cultural groups, religious groups, and interest groups – like those Meetup groups you would've been thinking about before.)

20. How much are lifestyles, attitudes, and values changing?

21. What opportunities are there in the values, subcultures, hobbies, and attitudes? (Think in terms of ways you could get "plugged in" to the community to raise money, forge new relationships, or become better advocates.)

Questions About Your Challenge

Concentration is important to creative thinking, problem analysis, and decision making. How exactly can concentration improve decision making and problem analysis? The general answer – by forcing you to think things through – should be obvious. When you are faced with an important decision try asking these questions, taken from *Why Didn't I Think of That?*

1. What might happen if I don't think this through completely?
2. What pressures – real or imagined – could force me to decide too quickly?
3. How will I prevent those pressures from sabotaging my thinking?

As you concentrate on a subject there are several steps to effective thinking that should be kept in mind. Set aside time to deliberate on the subject at hand. Make time in your schedule. The more serious the issue at hand the more time should be scheduled. You need to be ready to accept 100% responsibility for your thinking and its results. Understand the situation fully, by collecting data and talking to other people, before rushing into a decision.

Take a step back from the subject of your thinking and make sure you have framed the challenge correctly. Don't accept the first "frame" that comes to mind. A frame, just to review, is a perspective on a subject. Frames can include things like gender, poverty, lack of education, corruption, patriarchy, Marxism, and pretty much anything that tells us how to think about an issue. The problem of juvenile delinquency can be framed as a consequence of moral decline or as a result of persistent poverty. Do you think those two frames will produce different policy ideas?

Various social change or social betterment activities will have their own specific questions to ask. Those questions have to address the particulars of defining social or environmental problems and planning how to address those problems.

Advocacy groups may need to ask questions about the institutions, organizations, behaviors, and attitudes that wish to influence. Questions about norms, beliefs, economic arrangements, politics and technology might also be appropriate. A few specific examples should be useful, at least to inspire other appropriate questions:

1. Is there any parallel to this challenge in the business world?

2. Are there any social science principles or concepts we could apply?

3. What factors contributed to this social problem?

4. Can we attack the whole problem at once, or only address symptoms?

Education organizations whether they are schools or nonprofit education organizations, also have to ask specific questions about the social environment, students, clients, and students' families. A few examples of education questions indicate the specific types of questions that need to be asked.

1. What organizations, in any, have started a potentially useful program?

2. Who else may have tried to solve a similar education-related problem?

3. Are there any learning objectives that you overlooked?

Anyone planning a fundraising effort, with a specific objective, may want to ask some questions about the problem being addressed and the plan for addressing that problem one some money is raised. Maybe a different problem or a different approach is called for. Asking the right questions might just lead to a major change in plans. The questions could also strengthen confidence in the original plan. Maybe the answers will yield something you can use in a fundraising appeal. Consider a few sample questions that can be used to explore fundraising efforts.

1. How much money do we really need?

2. Can we substitute goods or services for some or all of the money?

3. Who may have tried to do so, and how did they do it?

Programs and policies need to be developed with due attention given both to the problem and to the plan for addressing the problem.

1. Have you seriously considered the logical connections between the policy or program and the issue to be addressed?

2. Have you verified that the policy or program justification is free of logical and factual errors?

3. Who may have dealt with a similar issue and how? Could all or part of the solution simply be copied?

To return to the chronic unemployment issue, program design might have to wait until some more questions have been answered. It might be helpful to ask around or do some research in case a similar community has dealt with similar problems. Always check your thinking for errors in logic and fact. That step should be obvious, but it helps to be reminded before committed resources to something that hasn't been worked through in detail.

Imagine it is one year from now (or imagine any other realistic time frame) and the problem or challenge you wanted to work on has been handled successfully. How could this have happened? What step came just before success, then just before that step, and before that and before that...? Go back as many steps as needed to get to where you are today. Now you know the next step to take. That piece of advice comes from Charles McCoy's book *Why Didn't I think of That?* and echoes the advice sometimes given about personal goal setting:

Imagine you have achieved your goal and work backward one step at a time to figure out what you should do next. McCoy has some other advice to offer: Exercise a vivid imagination. Imagine courageously. Imagine your way through any difficulty. Go beyond conventional wisdom and "common sense" as you look for an idea. Imagine the best possible solution. Use the "working backward" technique to figure out how that ideal solution could be brought about.

Two other questions come from *Why Not?* by Barry Naleboff and Ian Ayers. We all face limits on money and human resources. That doesn't mean we are obliged to think about ideas with our actual resources in mind, at least not all of the time. The first question is this - What would a consumer or leader with unlimited resources do to solve the problem?

Sometimes people cause social problems because they can pass along the costs of their bad behavior to other people. A classic example of this is the cost of driving a car - the true social and environmental impacts of driving aren't borne by the driver. The second question is this - How can people be made to pay the full social and environmental costs of their actions? In the driving example a higher gas tax would be one, admittedly unrealistic way, to force drivers to pay the full cost of driving.

Seeing the issue clearly and accurately is fundamental to solving a problem or improving a situation or making a sound decision. Most people know this but never use a formal method for improving their understanding of a situation. Of course most people don't make decisions that affect many other lives or involve huge sums of money (except for buying a home). The first step in perceiving a situation correctly and accurately is to gather data and to research expert opinions. Pay attention to the details, and not just the big picture or the obvious facts. Verify that your facts and assumptions are correct. In school many of us learned about the value of checking facts against a second source, or of going back to the original source to check a citation's validity.

The same sort of due diligence is called for in thinking about ways to improve society. It is not good enough to think that guns are the root cause of violence in your city. Decide on the crucial facts in a situation. Here are some questions to use in checking your perceptions of the issue:

1. What must be true, or false, for your solution/idea/innovation to work?
2. Do the facts support the viability of the idea?
3. Why will this idea work?
4. Why is the answer valid?
5. Are you focusing on a tree (one element) and ignoring the forest (the whole set of elements?
6. What other dimensions of the problem should you be thinking about?

Consider how these questions might be applied to understand chronic unemployment in the community. Maybe people need training in new skills, skills that your programs aren't addressing now. Do they know that? Do they know how to "sell" their new skills to prospective

employers? Are the people in question even employable? Is the lack of
basic jobs skills an issue for many people, or only a few? Most could
be immigrants whose command of English is poor, or many could have
substance abuse problems. In such situations, learning business writing
or conflict resolution may not be useful. That is a clear case of not
seeing the forest (unsuitability for employment) for the trees (one or
two specific challenges Ask tough questions: Use the 5 Why technique
to probe both the problem and the solution.

Social change involves marketing of some sort. People need to
be "sold" on an idea, a program or policy, the need to donate money, or
the need to alter some behavior. Before setting off to sell an idea a few
questions are in order:

1. What does your audience really want and how do you know?
2. What channels have others' used to advertise a similar message?

3. What benefit are you offering?
4. What are the benefits of the idea, for the audience?
5. Why should people believe in your idea?

Marketing in the social sector is not unlike marketing goods
and services for profit. People don't care about you or your cause; they
only care about their own needs and wants. Your audience will want to
know why they should put their faith in your organization and its
message.

Newspaper articles are supposed to describe the who, what,
where, when, why, and how of the story. Studying a social change

challenge can benefit from the same structure for thinking about a social change effort. Start with questions about the sources of the problem, or about the opportunity. What caused the problem or contributes to it? Where is the problem most prevalent and why? When do we need to act? When did the problem emerge? Who is most affected by the problem? Who can help us exploit this opportunity? What resources do we need to effectively tackle the problem? Which possible solutions for the problem are likely to work? Those are just some generic questions. Your specific circumstances should suggest other journalistic questions that apply. Identify those questions, answer them, and get better results.

Questions About Your Assumptions

According to Stanford Social Innovation Review, many activists and social entrepreneurs fall prey to the need equals demand fallacy. This fallacy is the false belief that because you see a clear need for a program, policy, or practice, there must be significant demand. Your city doesn't have a plastics recycling program, but people want to recycle their plastic. Therefore, you should mobilize people and money to create a program or pressure the city government to create one. The most important assumption you need to test might be the assumption that people want what you are selling.

Modification Questions – SCAMPER

Some challenges involve adapting, modifying or combining to create something new. There is a tool to help you with this. SCAMPER is an acronym for Substitute, Combine, Adapt, Magnify, Put to other uses, Eliminate, and Reduce. Each element of SCAMPER needs to be addressed separately.

What can you *substitute* in the current idea to make it work in your circumstances, or just to make it work better? Consider all parts of the idea – promotional methods, audience, medium, materials, resources (time for money, volunteers for staff), settings (greenhouses versus farms perhaps).

Elements of the idea can be *combined* with another idea in most cases. Innovations, programs, policies, and projects can all be combined in some way, at least in theory. The obvious objective here to find a useful and realistic combination. What combinations would work? What combinations are truly realistic given your resources and time frame available? What elements could be extracted and combined?

Most ideas have elements that can be *adapted* to another setting. What could you adapt to the realities of your organization, community, group, or local government? All ideas involve process, technologies, reward systems, or rules (formal or informal) that could be modified to work in other settings. Structures and processes invented somewhere else might be adapted to meet your organization's needs. Strategies and tactics for activism or public education can be borrowed from one setting and used in another setting. Strategies and tactics can be adapted from other types of campaigns with different objectives.

An idea may have a minor element that can be *maximized* or magnified to make the idea more suitable for your circumstances. The usual elements of an idea – geographic reach, audience, resources – can all be maximized or magnified. Could you take a small idea and make it into a big idea? Could you take any element of the idea and focus on making it bigger.

Can the idea be *put to other uses*? Maybe the whole idea can't be put to other uses, but some element can be. Could a marketing tactic be applied to a different cause? Could the idea be used within a cause but for a different objective or goal?

Maybe something in the idea you want to borrow can be *eliminated*. Could a part of the idea be dropped entirely? Can certain expenses be eliminated? Can the need to work in a particular setting or location be eliminated? Can any steps or stages be eliminated? Can a stage be eliminated?

A worthy idea may have one or two elements that need to minimized or *reduced* in some way. Maybe the amount of change or the geographic scope or another dimension can be scaled back to produce an idea that better fits your circumstances. The number of program participants and the number of seats in a class are two things that could be reduced. Advertising costs related to a new initiative can be minimized by relying on existing clients or students, on advertising in the organization's newsletter, or by advertising on the organization's Web site.

Part 2:

Six Steps to Better Results

5 – Study Your Challenge

Social service organizations, activists, schools, and government agencies all have challenges. If that were not true, the organization or group might not exist. A challenge can be a problem, in the usual sense, or just an opportunity that a group of people decide to act on.

A problem can be of two broad types. First, the performance of some system or process could be worse than expected for reasons that are not clear. Second, the outcomes might not be good enough.

Everyone has some informal problem-solving methods they use. We think about the subject. Maybe we can compare the current problem situation to similar situations we've encountered in the past. We can talk to colleagues. We can pore over data, maybe with some educated guess about what to find or what data is most relevant.

The informal problem solving process just outlined could be improved in several ways. Problem solving needs to be more formalized and systematic. This is so because the stakes are high in solving social problems. In organizations, an inaccurate assessment of the problem wastes resources that many nonprofits and activist groups cannot afford.

Problem solving efforts can be divided into two stages – structuring and analyzing. The structuring stage, collecting and organizing information always comes first. This stage may require nothing more than writing down a few already-known facts or numbers. Or, a relatively more sophisticated and formal process may be called for. This chapter offers a couple of tips on structuring problems and follows them with techniques for analyzing the problem.

Information Needs

You will probably have some information that is relevant to a problem. You can probably think of specific information that can help to solve the problem. Some focused thinking on what you need to know to deal with the problem at hand may reveal other information that's needed.

Edward de Bono created an attention-directing technique that makes it easier to identify information needs. FI-FO, inFormation In-inFormation Out, directs the user's attention to information that is available and information that is needed to solve a problem.

Make two lists of information needs. One list is for information that is on hand. The other list is basically a list of questions about missing facts. Going through the process of making that information list should make it easy to figure out what information is missing. Once those gaps are identified they can be addressed, and subsequent planning will be much more effective.

Data Collection

Several data collection techniques can contribute to successful problem analysis. Sometimes, maybe most of the time, we need to know how serious the problem is, for whom, and where the severity is less than average or more than average. The more complex the problem, the more people affected, or the greater the resource commitment called for by a solution the more important is formal and systematic data collection. Formal data collection implies a specific process will be followed. A formal process allows others to reproduce the data

This may be useful in gaining credibility for an analysis and the resulting solution you propose. If you are not going to be implementing the solution then you will need to sell the proposed solution. Whoever is expected to commit time and money to a solution will reasonably expect to see strong evidence and sound reasoning behind the proposed solution.

A systemic data collection method has specific and concrete steps to follow. Typically, data collection starts with a problem statement - What are the barriers to employment that homeless people and those on welfare face in this community? After the problem statement has been decided on, the actual data collection can begin. The next steps would be to list the information that you have and the information that's missing. This process should sound familiar. A strategy for collecting the missing information would be devised and implemented. Often, this will be just as easy as it seems.

Being systematic in collecting data on a social problem is critical for the same reason that some formality is critical: gaining credibility with the public, corporate executives, school administrators, or legislators.

Many problems in organizations don't require much data collection. You can look up a few facts, talk to a couple of people, and then come to a tentative conclusion about what needs to be done. In other cases, much more effort and formality will be required.

Understanding complex situations will require collecting many facts, dates, and numbers. You will need to identify sources of statistics, collect performance information, study records of class attendance or fundraising efforts (time spent versus money raised), and more. How much more depends on whether there is an internal problem with the organization's operations, or an external problem related to the organization's mission.

A couple of examples from the social sector should make it clear why data collection can sometimes, but not usually, require a major data collection effort. Persistent poverty in an area can be traced to several factors such as lack of education, geographic isolation from good jobs or good markets, and racism. Knowing the historical causes of a specific situation may be helpful, but you really need to know what's happening there now.

Why is the situation as bad as it is now? How do you know? Unless you take a systematic approach to answering that question your nonprofit's efforts will be less successful than they could be. Why don't more people recycle more of their household waste? Is it laziness, lack of recycling locations, lack of a concrete incentive, ignorance of area recycling locations, or lack of a program that makes recycling easy? Probably a combination of all factors is involved, but unless you investigate the matter you are only guessing.

Defining the point at which a problem is no longer a problem may also take some work. When is a recycling program a success? Do we want a 90% participation rate? What does that mean anyway? What is a reasonable increase in recycling – a 20% increase in the amount of plastic, glass, and metal being recycled? Is there an external standard of some sort, maybe recycling rates in a comparable European city? Will you simply pull a number out of the air? The same general questions could be applied to an attack on persistent poverty. How much poverty is acceptable? How much of a reduction in what time frame is realistic and how do you know?

Part of the data collection phase of problem analysis might require finding research that answers such questions. The point being to give a reasonable and defensible answer to the question: "What does success look like?" The answer could be used within the organization or to convince potential donors that you have a realistic and viable plan to address the problem in question.

Data Collection and Analysis

Collecting data and analyzing it might be beyond the capabilities of an individual or organization. Not knowing how to collect or analyze the information you need doesn't have to be a show-stopper.

One option is to ask for a graduate student to volunteer. Maybe that person needs a dissertation or thesis topic. He or she could do the research and analysis and share the results. This is a win-win situation.

Action Without Borders runs a Web site, www.idealist.org, where organizations can recruit volunteers. Try signing up and posting a description of your research project. If you don't have access to willing and able graduate student volunteers in your area, Idealist.org might be a good option.

A couple of do-it-yourself options are available. Maybe you only need to check some percentages or figures for a trend or a pattern. Either option is relatively easy using any spreadsheet software. Sometimes looking at counts, percentages, and proportions can paint a pretty good picture of the situation.

Chronologies

Sorting and listing events according to the order in which they occurred is a powerful and simple way to better understand a problematic situation. In *The Thinker's Toolkit* author Morgan Jones notes that our brains struggle to deal with disjointed facts and events. Therefore, we need to put things in some sort of order. This is what a chronology does.

The basic technique is simple enough to understand simply list all potentially relevant events in the order that they occurred. Start with the earliest event that seems relevant. Merely focusing on a sequence of events one at a time should reveal potential causes of a problem, or at least factors that contributed to the problem.

Once you have a few ideas about the potential cause of the problem, data collection, hypothesis testing, or other techniques can reveal whether your potential causes are indeed to blame. Use chronologies within the organization to diagnose problems with volunteers (recruitment efforts or retention), fundraising, programs, and projects. Why did things go bad, in whatever sense the word "bad" applied to the particular situation?

Five Why Technique

Problem analysis requires using some methodology to discover the root of the problem. Sopping up water with towels does not stop the toilet from leaking on the bathroom floor. Attacking a symptom of a social problem is not the same as trying to solve the problem. Sometimes the actual root of the problem may be unsolvable, as in human nature, the laws of physics, cultural or religious beliefs that are deeply entrenched.

The cause of the problem could be totally beyond the organization's ability to attack it. Maybe the real problem-solving goal here is to maneuver into a position where directly attacking the problem is more realistic. Doing so may mean acquiring more money, more staff, new skills, or new connections with other organizations.

In all three cases, the Five Why technique can help to better understand the situation. The technique is deceptively easy to use. State the problem. Ask why the situation exists. Ask why regarding that answer. Why does that thing, perception, belief, or situation exist? Ask why two or three more times. Why is it this way? Why does this happen? Why does it work this way? Why does this situation exist? Why does this perception still exist? Why does this belief still exist? You may not need to ask "why" five times to reach a new problem definition.

Stop asking when you get to an answer that doesn't seem to be a symptom of a deeper problem. Problems that you can think of, but that aren't amenable to change can't really be considered deeper problems. You aren't going to solve the "problem" of human greed. You might be able to mitigate or solve a problem that grows out of greed.

Simple Brainstorming

Some problems don't really need complicated formal analysis. However, thinking the cause(s) of a problem is (are) obvious does not mean anything. Some focused thinking about the problem is still a necessity. Take a few minutes to consider where the problem occurs, where it doesn't occur, when it occurs, when it doesn't occur, any events or conditions that are associated with the appearance of the problem.

Why do teenagers start smoking? Maybe they want to smoke. Maybe a genetic defect is responsible. Maybe peer pressure, lack of parental supervision, and relentless advertising pressure are involved.

A little rebelliousness may also contribute – adults hate for us to smoke so we need to smoke! Do a little brainstorming on the same subject and you may come up with one or two other contributing factors. The important question to ask at the end of a brainstorming session is this: Which of those contributing factors are realistically in our power to influence? In the case of teen smoking we may be able to use peer pressure to discourage teenagers from picking up the nicotine habit.

Hypothesis Testing

How do we think X and Y are related? That is the basis of hypothesis testing. A hypothesis is an informed guess about the relationships between two variables: Scientists would use a theory to derive a hypothesis. Informally, common sense or current knowledge about an issue like chronic homelessness should be enough.

Consider an example of hypothesis testing applied to social activism. There is a strong, positive relationship between education level of parents and their children. This simple hypothesis could be tested by surveying people to see what level of education they have attained and what level each parent obtained. Statistical testing will reveal the nature and strength of any relationship between parent and child educational attainment.

Hypothesis testing has a broader role in solving social problems and various management problems. The process works somewhat differently than it does in social science research. We state that the presence of one condition, or its absence, is associated with the problem. This is more like answering a yes/no question that a process of measuring the strength and direction of a statistical relationship. Remember that this is only a structuring technique that helps the user to

Consider two types of evidence in hypothesis testing: Evidence that's available, evidence that's missing but would support one of the hypotheses, and missing evidence that would refute one of the hypotheses. The specific question to ask is this: What evidence not included in the matrix would refute one or more of the hypotheses?

For general problem-solving purposes a bit less rigor is acceptable. All you need to do is state your hypothesis or hypotheses, as in the teenage deviance example, and look for data that tests the hypothesis. For instance, the number of family dinners each week could be something that's available in published surveys. Somebody has almost certainly done some scholarly research on the relationship between family time and teen deviance. All you need to do is locate the research and see what the researchers concluded. Published statistics from the United States Census Bureau, the United States Bureau of Labor Statistics, the United Nations, and many other sources could give you all the information you need to check your hypothesis.

Phoenix Checklist

The U.S. Central Intelligence Agency created a list of questions that its agents could use as an aid to solving problems. Michael Michalko lists the basic questions and describes their application to creative problem solving in his book *Thinkertoys*. The Phoenix questions actually consist of two lists of questions, one for examining the problem and one for planning a solution. The lists that follow present a version of the Phoenix Checklist, with many items added or modified to reflect a social change focus.

1. Why is it necessary to solve the problem?
2. What benefits will you receive from solving the problem?
3. Do you have enough information to solve the problem?
4. What information is missing, incomplete, or contradictory?
5. Is this problem like anything you've seen before?
6. How urgent is it that you solve the problem?
7. What skills, talents, and equipment will you need to use?
8. What social conditions seem to be contributing to the problem?
9. Can you find a similar problem that's already been solved?
10. Could you adapt the solution to a different but related problem?
11. What might happen if the problem persists?
12. Can you break the problem down into component parts?

Making a Plan

1. Can you solve the whole problem at once?
2. What would the ideal solution look like?
3. How close can you come in real life to that ideal solution?
4. What characteristics must a realistic solution possess?
5. Who needs to do what?
6. What needs to be done first?
7. What assumptions do you have about your planned solution?
8. Have you checked the validity of those assumptions?
9. Who will be responsible for implementing the solution?
10. What steps are involved in designing and implementing a solution?
11. What tools need to be employed to help solve this problem?

12. How will you track progress in implementing a solution?

13. How will you know you have successfully solved the problem?

14. Have you accounted for all of the requirements of a good solution?

What laws, political conditions, economic realities, technologies, and cultural norms need to be accounted for? Those are the sorts of things that should come up while answering questions 4, 7, 8, and 14.

The Kepner-Tregoe Method

Kepner and Tregoe developed a problem analysis method for the business world. The method is appropriate for social problems as well. In Kepner-Tregoe terminology a problem is any situation in which an expected level of performance is not being achieved for a reason that is currently unknown. If fewer people are enrolling in your nonprofit's classes this may or may not qualify as a problem. A correct problem statement is one that calls for a situation to be investigated rather than calling for a decision to be made. Consider these two examples:

1. "We've been working to raise more funds for three weeks, but we've only raised half as much as last year at the same time. What went wrong?

2. Our fundraising drive only raised 80% as much as expected. What are we going to do now?

The first example was a problem statement because it expresses awareness of a deviation in performance from what was expected.

They expected to have raised more money by this point. The cause of the deviation is unknown or else there would be no reason to ask what went wrong. The second example simply specifies the deviation and asks for a yes or no answer to a question. The second question could be rephrased like the first one: What went wrong this time?

Problem analysis is a six-step process that always begins with a *problem statement.* The statement "We've been working to raise more funds for three monthss, but we've only raised half as much as last year." This is a statement of one problem; a shortfall in funds raised, and does not contain an explanation of why the deviation is occurring.

A correct problem statement does not contain a solution and does not identify the source of the problem. To create a problem statement you must name only one problem, a problem that does not have an identifiable source. The source doesn't even have to be a proven source, only one that is highly plausible. Stating that fundraising is way down this year because of gas prices would not be plausible and would beg the question of whether there really is a relationship between the high gas prices and the reduced fundraising results.

The next step in problem analysis is to *specify the problem.* Specifying a problem requires answering four sets of questions about the problem.

1. Where is the subject when the deviation is observed? (applies when there are multiple sites or locations involved in the process being studied.)
2. Where is the deviation in the process?
3. What is the specific deviation? What specific process or sub-

process has the deviation?

4. When did the deviation occur? Is there any pattern evident?

5. How big is the deviation? How many group, sites, locations, sub-processes, projects, programs have the deviation? How big is each deviation? How many deviations are there in each group or site.

A return to the problem with fundraising will illustrate how these questions can be posed and answered in problem analysis. Assume that the fundraising effort is on the same scale as last years' effort and has the same approach. You mailed letters to our in-house mailing list. You hired a firm to make some fundraising calls. You placed hundreds of post cards in a couple of dozen area businesses. You also paid for six small ads in six consecutive Sunday editions of the main daily newspaper. When the deviation in fundraising results became clear, three of the six ads had been placed. So, the deviation appeared when we were less than half finished with this year's big fundraising effort.

We have to ask where the deviation first appeared. Did one of our three fundraising tools come up well short of expectations? Of course, we would need to know what each tool yielded three weeks into last years' campaign. We would also want to find out if there was a sudden drop in results with any or all three methods. Maybe all three were doing badly from the very beginning. In any case we will want to look at the size of the deviation and the extent of it for each fundraising method.

A careful investigation of the what, where, when, and how much questions for each of the fundraising methods could reveal something like the summary shown below:

1. *Where?*   In returns from direct mail letters and fundraising calls.

2. *What?* Drop in fundraising results, compared to same time frame and same methods used last year.

3. *When?* Noticed in week 3, appeared in week 2, insignificant difference noted in week 1.

4. *How much?* 60% for direct mail, 0% from newspaper ads, 50% from fundraising calls.

The next questions cover where the deviation is and is not occurring. These questions will be relatively easy to answer since some of the information had to be collected to present the answers shown in Table 2. The deviation could be occurring in all methods but is actually occurring in direct mail (down 60%) and fundraising calls (down 50%). We can also answer the "how much" question by noting the percentage of decline in results for each of the methods. We know that the deviation first appeared in week two, though a minor deviation occurred in week one. That first week's small deviation is not enough to merit further attention in a good year. It is too early to try to establish a trend. With a six-week fundraising effort it isn't practical to wait for the information that would be needed to establish a trend.

In the next problem analysis step we look for anything that's different in this year's fundraising efforts compared with last years' work. What changed in the direct mail effort, in the telephone effort, in the letter, in or the content of the telephone appeal? What changed in the mailing list or in the calling list used for the telephone fundraising? Was there a change of any sort in the telephone fundraising organization, i.e., to a new organization? Did the old organization change hiring practices, training, or anything else that may have affected results?

More generically we can specify a problem by asking more questions about the location, group, program, project, or process. What is distinctive about the staff, participants, location, resources, or time frame that may be contributing to the deviation? And what about the areas where the deviation is not occurring? The same factors need to be considered and specified to reach some conclusion about the observed deviations.

You also need to ask what changed at about the same time the deviation appeared. Any change in setting, people, technology, resources, or social environment could account for the deviation. The only way to find out is to examine those things to see what may have changed.

You need to *test possible causes* against the problem specification. Start by listing possible causes of the deviation. Determine whether the cause could really have contributed to the deviation in question. In all cases the potential causes of a deviation need to be tested by asking how the cause would have resulted in the observed deviation. In the fundraising example it might be true that the fundraising firm did something that affected results. Maybe a much-less rigorous hiring and training program was instituted to cut costs. The new staff is not as committed or as skilled as last year's telephone staff. This possibility can be investigated by quizzing the management at that company.

Maybe the direct mail results are really a distinct problem. We still want to explain the big drop in results from those direct mail pieces. This could be part of a larger problem; a fundraising strategy that wasn't changed to match changes in the social environment of our organization. It would certainly be reasonable to divide up the "fundraising effort" into direct mail, newspaper advertising, and telephone soliciting components. Now have three different deviations to analyze, perhaps with one staff member working on each.

The next problem analysis step is to *determine the most likely cause* of the deviation. The direct mail could be going to people with a flagging interest in charitable giving or have more financial problems than the general public. Maybe a skilled copywriter didn't write the new letter. Assuming the letter is good and the mailing list is good, one has to look at changing economic conditions as a realistic explanation.

The decline in results from telephone solicitations could have several explanations. The change in training and hiring was already mentioned. The company may be using an overused list of phone numbers. Maybe the company is using random digit dialing instead of using a list of people with a known interest in relevant issues.   Did you fail to provide a good list this year? Did they fail to rent a good list, as they claimed they would do in their contract? After establishing a likely cause, we need to monitor that cause or try a fix and see what happens.

Selling the Analysis

Selling an analysis of the problem may be necessary. You may not be able to solve the problem yourself. You may not be in a group that has gone through the process together and come to an agreement about the cause of a problem. Or, the problem could be too demanding of time and resources. In any of these situations you really have a two-part task: figure out how to sell the analysis, then sell the analysis.

Figuring out how to sell an analysis is a matter of combining status, persuasiveness, statistics, and logic to create a compelling case. There is no magic here and no secrets. You simply need to use persuasive writing and knowledge of your audience.

Selling an analysis also means considering the people who are supposed to be "buying" the analysis. In the social sector, the buyers are often voters, politicians, or potential donors. They need to be sold on your analysis of the issue. There is no substitute for either direct experience working with the people in question, or for market research. Without one or the other, the selling job could prove impossible.

Problem Analysis in Activism

Problem analysis works best when the situation is quantifiable. Collecting signatures on a petition, raising money, and attracting people to rallies or protests are all "activist" things with quantifiable outcomes. We can readily tell if our efforts are meeting expectations. That assumes you defined a realistic and measurable goal. Activists can try to influence an opinion that's been measured by a scientifically valid survey or poll. Maybe nothing goes wrong and the activists in question are happy with their results. Maybe a follow-up survey suggests that the group's social marketing effort hasn't been doing much good. This is where problem analysis comes in handy. We can employ a systematic process to look at where the deviation in performance is or is not. What types of people aren't responding as expected? Where do those people live and what characteristics do they share? Even better: Is there any evidence pointing to a reason for your idea not "selling" to them.

Problem Analysis in Fundraising

Fundraising campaigns don't always work as expected. You might not get that grant proposal, but those one-off events aren't really "problems" in the sense used in this chapter. An ongoing campaign that isn't producing good results is a problem – there is a deviation from expected performance and the cause of the deviance is unknown. The same comments apply to efforts at soliciting in-kind contributions. If things are going badly, you obviously want to test possible explanations of the lack of contributions. Don't guess that the economy is bad or the city is poor. Don't assume that people know why the issue is important and why the project you're doing is important. It might be obvious to you but a complete mystery to John and Jane Doe.

Problem Analysis in Policy and Program Design

Social policies and social programs usually have quantifiable results. If the real social benefits can't be readily quantified you can at least measure the outputs, such as the number of people who complete a money management course. A problem exists if the results aren't as expected. An even bigger problem exists if the results, or performance standards, required by the government or by an external funder aren't as required.

Two questions are relevant for policies and programs: What are the expected results? What is the nature of the deviation from expected results? When you can precisely specify the expected results, you can measure the deviation from that "standard" and know whether a problem exists. Why is the high school dropout rate still 54%? If the national average is 10%, there is a clear measure of how big the deviation really is.

Professional Help

Consultants, seminars, and college courses are always choices to consider. Consultants specializing in solving complex business problems may have experience with nonprofits or with social change work Trainers can teach certain problem solving skills, including Direct Attention Thinking Tools (DATTT ®) and Kepner-Tregoe methods.

Taking a college course may not be the first or even second thing that comes to mind. However, many courses on evaluation research, statistics, qualitative research, and survey research can actually help you study a problem and track your success in addressing the problem. Almost all colleges and universities offer introductory courses on statistics and survey research. Some schools also offer courses on evaluation research, qualitative research methods, and advanced topics in statistics or research methods. The disadvantage of college and university courses is the time and money required for the course after applying to the school, of course.

If taking a class is too much of an investment, you could always start by reading a book. Simple books on statistical analysis, research methods, and survey research all exist. Even used undergraduate textbooks from an online bookstore will give you enough information for most research tasks that the average nonprofit or school will face. If you want to use the Internet for research there are even books on using the Web for survey research and a few titles on using the Internet for general research, i.e. looking things up.

6 – Problems and Opportunities

Social betterment involves more than simple problem solving. Solving problems can be devilishly hard in the politically and ideologically charged social sector. Problem solving is still just one thing. What about improving existing services, processes, or programs? What about looking for opportunities to take advantage of? What about foreseeing problems and opportunities so your organization can be for them?

Many people solve problems, improve things, *and* look for problems and opportunities. Being able to use a formal process for identifying potential threats or potential opportunities may give better results. You are less likely to miss something important. Informal investigation and reflection could yield an adequate understanding of the organization's current social environment.

A systemic process to gather and analyze information about possible future events may be helpful. Environmental scanning through content analysis is one such process. Kepner-Tregoe developed another technique called situation appraisal, described in this chapter and applied to the nonprofit world.

Environmental Scanning

Looking out for potential problems and potential opportunities may not be that difficult. Anyone who pays attention to news affecting the community or chosen issue is doing environmental scanning. The objective in this section is to teach a couple of systematic techniques you could apply to make environmental scanning more fruitful, more efficient, or both.

Sociological research on organizations yields 21 elements of the social environment that might bear watching. This sociological model of organizations divides the social environment into seven dimensions – ecological, legal, demographic, technological, political, economic, and cultural. Each of those dimensions has three characteristics – capacity, resources, and dynamism (rate of change.

You could easily ask a question about each cell in that table. In fact that is the recommended way to use those combinations of dimensions and characteristics. Some sample questions, and the "cell" in Table 4 that's reflected, will get your imagination working:

1. What is the rate of change in the population we serve? (demographic dynamism)
2. How many sources of financial support can we identify? (economic complexity)
3. How much financial support is available for nonprofit organizations (economic capacity) What new technologies should we be looking at now? (technological capacity)
4. How are those technologies changing? (technological dynamism)

It might be helpful to create a table similar to Table 2 and fill in the cells with answers that are specific to your own organization or group. You will want to follow a systematic methodology for scanning the environment. One commonly used method borrowed from the social sciences is all that you really need. The following table summarizes the dimensions of the social environment and their characteristics.

Dimensions of the Social Environment and Characteristics

	complexity	dynamism	capacity
ecological			
economic			
Demographic			
Legal			
political			
Technologica l			
cultural			

Content Analysis

How do you actually do an environmental scan? Another social science tool called content analysis can help us to identify trends or patterns in society. The basics of content analysis are relatively simple to learn. Keep the following four steps in mind:

1. Know likely sources of information – consider sources for information on technology, economics, politics, legal issues, environmental issues, and demographic issues that might be relevant to your group or organization.

2. Know the sorts of statistics or themes that relate to your organization's social environment.

3. Write things down - Keep track of what gets mentioned and how often. Make notes on statistics and on events.

4. Pay attention to what's missing. What doesn't get covered may reflect ideological biases that you need to be aware of,

assuming the bias could become a problem for your organization.

The preceding four steps aren't exactly a rigorous data collection method, but a simple and workable method is all that we really need.

The point of all this reading, note taking, and thinking is to paint a detailed picture of the sorts of threats and opportunities that you'll want to consider in your planning. Content analysis can also help in evaluating the current and future value of an existing program or policy.

A short example using renewable energy, will make the process clearer. A nonprofit might be focused on promoting wide user of solar power technology in homes and businesses. Federal, state, and local policies could all influence demand for solar power technology. Tax incentives or free training on how to install and maintain the equipment come to mind. *Proposed* federal, state, or local government policies related to renewable energy technology are important. Economic analysis of the technology – how much it costs versus the savings – would be useful. Social marketing efforts and demonstration projects by government agencies, companies, or nonprofits could happen. Public opinion research on renewable energy technology could yield a better understanding of how to "sell" your organization's ideas.

Potential Problem/Potential Opportunity Analysis

These two tools also come from the consulting from of Kepner-Tregoe. Potential problem analysis and potential opportunity analysis are used separately but follow the basic steps outlined here:

1. Determine the end result or goal of the action to be undertaken.

2. List potential problems or opportunities that may result.

3. Consider possible causes for each potential problem?

4. Take action to reduce the odds of the problem appearing or to make the opportunity more likely to appear.

5. Prepare actions to reduce the harm from potential problems or to take advantage of any opportunities that arise.

6. Set up a system for monitoring a situation so developing problems or opportunities are detected.

That's the basic and abstract description of how potential problem/potential opportunity analysis works. Both techniques are related in that each is future-focused. The only real difference is in focusing on undesirable events or desirable events. The following paragraphs supply some public sector examples of how to implement each step.

Suppose that we want to start a new organization devoted to educating the American public about lifestyle changes that we can make to combat global climate change. What foreseeable events would present problems or opportunities? How will we know when a problem or opportunity occurs? How will we know how to respond? What contingency plans can we make? Potential problem/potential opportunity analysis helps people answer those questions.

Any start-up organization is going to have personnel challenges and financial challenges and logistical challenges. Most such challenges can be anticipated and handled without any special "thinking tools" at one's disposal. Specialized tools can be helpful when big and expensive or big and valuable opportunities need to be identified and prepared for. These two steps are also important in creating a new organization. What could go wrong here? What opportunities do we need to be prepared for? How do we prepare?

We should start the analysis by deciding exactly what we want to accomplish. Establishing the organization is not the goal; it is only an interim objective. What we really want is to change people or organizations, or both, in specific and measurable ways. Should we focus on one change or on several related changes? Assume the organization only wants to make one change in peoples' minds: We want people to choose renewable energy sources for their home electricity, cooking, and heating needs. That goal really involves several changes in peoples' minds, one for each of the three areas and maybe one more for each realistic alternative.

What problems does our goal seem to suggest could appear? Consider what's happening in the economy, with the federal government, and with the mass media. What if gas and fuel oil prices drop significantly? While this seems unlikely, we could consider what happens to our "green energy" message if crude oil prices and coal prices 10-15% in the coming months. Public interest in actually using renewable energy sources, as opposed to reading about them may not be low to begin with. Interest can only drop with dropping energy prices. Pointing out the people that they aren't paying the full social and environmental costs of that fossil fuel use will not help. Money we "should" be paying is not as motivating as is the real money going out of our checking accounts.

The oil, coal, and natural gas industries could launch a public relations campaign to make renewable energy sources seem unattractive. They could do this by painting oil or coal as good, domestic sources of energy. We are talking about public relations here and not about science or economics. The unreality of such claims only matters if the abuse of facts or logic can be used against an industry.

So, a public relations effort by the oil industry would represent both a problem and an opportunity. Launching a "counterattack" will call for some creative thinking in development of a counter-message and in execution of a public relations effort.

Other things can go wrong with our renewable energy campaign. Federal energy policy could be revised, as it is regularly. Odds are good that any pending changes would favor oil, coal, and natural gas production. This policy shift is likely to be immune to influence by our budding nonprofit. So, what can be done? This is an issue that may need to be dealt with later by using brainstorming techniques or lateral thinking.

After we launch our renewable energy campaign, some opportunities are sure to present themselves. Maybe a prominent scientific organization publishes a report calling for aggressive consumer adoption of solar power technology. This report can lend credibility to our advice to homeowners. Maybe a few state governments will decide to offer grants for individuals to convert vehicles to run on E85 (a mixture of grain alcohol and gasoline). Even though E85 isn't truly renewable it does have a large renewable component. Our organization could start a campaign to make people aware of the program and help them decide to make the switch to E85. Maybe people need to know where they can buy the fuel and where they can get the conversions done professionally.

When to Use Potential Problem/Potential Opportunity Analysis

Potential problem/potential opportunity analysis (PP/PO)

should be applied whenever you start a new project, program, activism campaign or organization. New projects bring risks, and opportunities specific to the type of project in question. Look for potential problems and opportunities before beginning the project and during the project. This is one of the basic principles of good project management.

How do you use PP/PO in a project? Consider the areas of potential opportunity and risk that are always present in any project: time, money, people (specifically their skills or specialized knowledge), facilities, and equipment. These areas of risk and opportunity tend to be connected. If you lose a person or two it might be impossible to complete the project on time. Nonprofits obviously face the same problem – people quit or get fired or retire. Money may run out more quickly than expected because one phase of the project takes longer than expected. In either case the project will simply fail, or cost more, or will have to be scaled back. The facility you need might end up being shared with another project or group. Likewise, a piece of equipment may not be available as expected because of breakdowns or higher-priority projects. Both of those difficulties are common in business.

Projects in nonprofit settings can be derailed because of facility or equipment problems. A deal to use donated or cheaply leased space for an education program can fall through entirely. Is your project dependent on facilities or equipment provided by others? What about volunteer labor versus staff time? Perhaps some enthusiastic people will decide to "gamble" on having funds that haven't materialized yet. This can happen when people get excited about a project and just decide that the money issue will take care of itself with some fundraising or a grant proposal.

Nonprofit projects can be undermined by equipment problems.

What happens if the cargo van, the old and well-traveled cargo van, eats a piston in the middle of the project? Is there a way to repair the engine or get some alternate transportation? What if the project is more successful than anticipated and you don't have enough classroom space or computers to accommodate your prospective students? A nice problem to have! Still, a prudent person would try to anticipate that event and plan for it. Being swamped by people you could have planned to accommodate, but did not, can be a serious blow to your reputation.

In the business world, a project can be derailed or killed by competition or by senior management's changing priorities. Sometimes priorities change for good business reasons. Sometimes priorities change because an executive became sold on some new method, technique, or technology.

In the social sector projects have competition of two sorts. The organization's other activities need resources. Competition from other organizations or causes is also a reality. Other things are always competing for peoples' time and money. "Business as usual" is also a competitor in some cases.

If your project involves selling a new idea or new behavior to other people you face competition from the status quo. People don't like change because it is scary, stressful or a threat to someone's power. Industry groups or partisan political groups might oppose your project. How will the National Rifle Association react to your project aimed at banning handgun ownership in the city? On the positive side, what individuals or groups could you recruit as allies? How do you reach them and "convert" them to your cause?

Any nonprofit project or program will bring certain opportunities, opportunities that may not be at all obvious when things are just getting started. Potential opportunity analysis will help you uncover those opportunities and decide how or if to deal with them. What contingency plan can you make? How will you detect that new opportunity when it appears?

Situation Appraisal

Another Kepner-Tregoe tool, situation appraisal, makes it easier to stay in on the alert for problems and for opportunities. Situation appraisal is a framework for problem analysis, decision analysis, and for potential problem/potential opportunity analysis. So, the tools described in this chapter, the chapter on problem analysis, and the chapter on decision analysis can all be applied within the situation appraisal framework. An example follows a detailed description of the situation appraisal process.

Situation appraisal is a continuous 5-step process. The first activity is to list the threats and opportunities that an organization faces. The second step is to identify all separate concerns related to threats to the organization. Step three is evaluating the seriousness, urgency, and priority of each concern. The fourth step is to consider the type of analysis and amount of analysis needed to address the concern. The final step is to determine what sort of help is needed to deal with each concern. Then the situation appraisal process begins again; new threats and opportunities are always emerging.

Identifying threats and opportunities is the first step in situation appraisal. This process begins by focusing on a specific subject or time frame. Maybe the anticipated life span of a project is three years. What problems or opportunities seem likely to emerge?

The second step is to list known deviations from the expected results, any currently known threats, and any currently known opportunities.

Step three is to conduct a systematic search for possible threats and opportunities. The social environment always contains threats and opportunities that originate in political conditions, economic conditions, the law, changing technology, changing lifestyles and norms, or demographic changes. Finally, look for opportunities to improve the situation. Any program, organization, or project could use resources more efficiently or could identify ways to acquire new resources or ways to increase effectiveness.

In the next step, you identify all concerns they have about the program, project, or new organization. Kepner and Tregoe suggest a list of questions that should be asked about any situation:

1. Is there one action we can take to resolve this concern?
2. Is this concern really one thing or a set of narrower, related concerns?
3. Do we agree on the reason for our concern?
4. What evidence suggests this concern is really a concern?
5. Do we understand everything that is happening related to this concern?
6. What tells us we must take action to address this concern?
7. What actions does this concern indicate that we need to take?
8. How could we improve our handling of this situation?
9. What is really troubling us about this situation?

Answering these questions will call for research, conversations with coworkers, and some brainstorming. Some brainstorming is certainly going to be useful to deal with questions 1, 7 and 8.

Regarding question 2, a concern with low enrollment in a program could really encapsulate concerns about content, advertising, need, and teaching philosophy. Decision analysis could help answer question 7.

Concerns each need to be evaluated to decide how they need to be handled. Not all concerns are equally important, even if they may seem so at first. A systematic process for evaluating concerns should produce a better allocation of resources. The first step in evaluating concerns is to consider how each concern rates in each of three dimensions:

1. How *serious* is the concern in terms of its impact on people, reputation, clients, resources, or environmental quality?
2. How *urgent* is it that you act on a concern to keep things from getting worse?
3. What evidence is there that the concern will *grow* more serious?

Each concern can be ranked qualitatively as high, medium, or low. Any concern that ranks high in all three dimensions calls for immediate attention.

Classifying each concern will call for research on each of those three questions. The degree of impact and area(s) of impact will both need to be investigated through analyzing data, collected and analyzing new data, or conducting interviews. Data collection is the only way to verify that the concern is getting more serious or less serious. Research will also help you understand how quickly the concern may graduate from being moderate to very serious. With all of that information in hand it becomes much easier to prioritize and correctly allocate resources to various concerns.

After studying and prioritizing concerns decisions will need to be made regarding the type of analysis that's needed to resolve each concern. Here, other Kepner-Tregoe tools can be used in conjunction with lateral thinking tools or other methods of generating ideas. Planning might require doing a CAF on the factors influencing the chances of success. Consequence and Sequel or Other Peoples' Views can help to understand the likely outcomes for a plan. In the former case, the plan will have certain impacts over time, sometimes including unexpected or undesirable impacts. In many cases people will be expected to respond in some way, by signing up for classes, supporting a ballot initiative, donating money, or making a specific change in their lives. It is naïve to think changes and support will be forthcoming because they "make sense" in some sense.

If the situation in question requires further analysis and exploration a number of tools, are available. Simply scanning your own experience or talking to other knowledgeable people may be all that is necessary. The Kepner-Tregoe problem analysis technique is likely to be called for in many cases. A relatively simple form of hypothesis testing is enough in other cases. If you have the data you need already, then a hypothesis test may involve asking a simple yes or no question. Do the data support my hypothesis or not?

Sometimes no problem analysis is necessary because the cause of a deviation is known. The question changes from "What is the source of this problem?" to "What is different here?" The difference between settings where a deviation occurs and where the deviation doesn't occur can be useful information. Maybe you can attack the circumstances that led to different outcomes in one situation. An effort to organize protests in several cities results in significantly higher turnout in one city despite similar demographics. Why did the one city have higher turnout? Maybe that city had a municipal government holiday on the day in question? Maybe, in spite of similar demographics, that particular city has more well educated 18-29 year olds That demographic group tends to be relatively active and progressive.

Maybe your organization faces several options in planning projects, seeking funds, forming partnerships, or in some other strategic decision. The correct course of action will not always become obvious after a little thinking. Even in those cases, it might be helpful to spell out the reasons for picking one option as opposed to any of the others. Decision analysis techniques can help out here.

Situation appraisal, or elements of it, should be built into the plans for any new organization, project, or program. The tools can also be put to use in an ongoing program or project to produce better monitoring and control of activities. Finally, one or more of the situation appraisal steps could be used in regular appraisals of the organization's activities.

Situation appraisal can also be useful in different ways for different types of activities. Advocacy, education, fundraising, policy creation, program design, social services, social innovation, and strategy development could all be improved by incorporating situation appraisal. In no case is it absolutely necessary to use all of the steps in situation appraisal.

Advocacy

Making social change happen is partly an emotional effort but calls for planning and rational calculation of what can be done in what time frame with the available resources. Situation appraisal could be integrated into the work of any advocacy organization or activist group.

What threats and opportunities does your group need to deal with? How do you know? Environmental scanning and SWOT analysis can help identify both threats and opportunities. Other organizations, those with opposing agendas, are an obvious threat. Strategic alliances with other nonprofits or with businesses are always two opportunities worth watching for.

What concerns do you have about the prospects for your advocacy effort? These concerns could grow out of the previously identified threats or from other factors.   Access to money, equipment, resources, workers, and the media are all potential areas of concern for advocacy efforts. People may not respond well to what seems to the activists a perfectly reasonable proposal. Maybe a poor reception for your idea is a legitimate concern. What can be done about this?

Situation appraisal draws attention to specific areas where problem solving and brainstorming might be necessary. Potential problem/opportunity analysis will reveal areas where problems are likely or where opportunities may appear. Environmental scanning will also reveal likely problems or opportunities. What will you do to get ready for those opportunities? Creative thinking might be called for. Even simple techniques, like deciding to concentrate on generating ideas, may help prepare activists for action should a potential opportunity actually appear. Analyzing concerns about the group's goals and tactics and strategy will be invaluable in deciding how to allocate resources. In the likely event an organization is already well established when someone introduces situation appraisal analyzing concerns can reveal better ways to allocate resources.

Education

Schools have the same sorts of challenges as other organizations, at least in the abstract. On a concrete level, educators and administrators in all types of schools need to prepare for likely problems (and opportunities one would think), impending decisions, and they have to deal with current problems.

Adult education programs, school systems, and nonprofits that focus on education all need to use something like situation appraisal. All of those organizations have potential problems or opportunities to deal with. Being ready to solve the problems or exploit the opportunities only makes good sense. Managers, educators, and administrators need to study their concerns (current or potential problems) and consider how those concerns can be broken into manageable parts. Or, maybe the best approach is to simply take the concern at once. Situation appraisal can prepare you to deal with those concerns, to separate out their components, and to evaluate them.

Fundraising

Fundraising campaigns can be a long-term commitment to a cycle of special events, fundraising letters, and possibly other activities. Planning to raise money will be helped with situation appraisal techniques. Some questions are common to fundraising efforts: What tactics should we use? What is our goal? How should we sue the money? That last question is really a broader question of strategy and not exactly a fundraising question. However, knowing your specific goal or the relevant interim objective will indicate how much money to raise and probably what the time frame is for reaching that goal.

Those questions reflect the greatest threat and the greatest opportunity in fundraising. The tactics you use may be informed by opportunities. Is Earth Day coming up? An environmental group could obviously capitalize on that event to raise some extra money. The Earth Day example seems obvious but indicates the possibility that many non-obvious options are overlooked. A systematic process for evaluating threats and opportunities may help to reveal those overlooked options.

Creating and Selling Policies

Policies have to be created and sold whether politicians or activists are the authors. Activists may have a harder selling job. They have to convince and apathetic and potentially hostile audience to care about a particular issue. Enough people have to care for politicians to start paying attention, or for a policy idea to make it on the next ballot. In either situation a sustained effort is going to be necessary. This means an organizational effort that's substantial enough to use the whole situation appraisal process may be necessary. Parts of the process will always be useful. How do you know when to use problem analysis, potential problem/potential opportunity analysis, decision analysis, or the whole process of situation appraisal?

Problem analysis is still valuable whenever there is a deviation in performance of unknown cause. Maybe progress on getting petition signatures is worse than expected at the halfway point. Problem analysis will help reveal the source of the problem, or a simple hypothesis test may reveal the cause of the shortfall. You probably know enough about petition drives to make educated guesses about why people aren't responding. If the petition drive is happening in several cities, maybe problem analysis is a better choice than simple hypothesis testing. Many more factors can be involved with multiple locations. Hypothesis testing works best when one factor can be compared across locations or when two locations can be compared directly.

In the beginning of a petition drive it may make sense to do a formal study of potential threats and opportunities. As activities proceed you can monitor the social environment to see what threats or opportunities are really materializing. Deciding on the indicators to track would have been part of the potential problem/potential opportunity analysis. Concerns about volunteer labor, about getting enough signatures, or about running out of money need to be examined. Is the concern about volunteer labor really a set of related concerns that could be more effectively dealt with one at a time? Probably.

The next task is to determine how serious each concern is, how urgent it is, and how likely each is to grow in magnitude. Decide what sort of analysis is required to better understand the concerns involved. Do you need to decide between options, analyze a problem, or look for potential opportunities and threats? Another huge petition drive might be getting underway while your own petition drive is happening. The other petition drive could reduce the amount of labor you can get out volunteers. What sort of help might be needed to recruit volunteers and keep them in the face of competition for their discretionary time? Maybe you have the knowledge or skill needed to solve the problem. Maybe professional help is called for.

Program Design

Programs, including public education, social service, and others need to be planned, monitored, and modified sometimes. Sometimes some troubleshooting becomes necessary. Why are our results not what we expected? What factors in the program, in the audience, or in the social environment are involved?

At this point hypothesis testing may suffice to give an answer. The relatively involved Kepner-Tregoe method of problem analysis will be needed in some cases. Hypothesis testing is sufficient when you have one setting to work with and against which you can test an idea. If two or more groups need to be compared and tested for a specific difference, or several differences one at time then hypothesis testing can also work. When there are multiple possible causes and you don't even have an educated guess about the source of the problem, then problem analysis the circumstances call for problem analysis.

The whole situation appraisal process could be implemented at the same time a new program gets started. Then the beginning questions, about potential threats and potential opportunities are most salient. At the earliest stage of a program, perhaps when the program is still just a good idea, a potential problem/potential opportunity analysis can be valuable. What threats or opportunities might technology, demographic change, cultural norms, economic conditions, or the political climate present? How will you know if a particular threat or opportunity has emerged? Don't discount the possible impact of competing programs whether they are run by the local government or by another nonprofit program.

Decision analysis might help in prioritizing concerns. Sometimes one of two or three possibilities will be difficult to prioritize because they are so similar in likelihood and impact. The Kepner-Tregoe method of problem analysis may help you make a decision.

Social Innovation

Creating a non-technological solution to a problem seems like an obvious strategy to many activists. Creating a non-technological way to exploit an opportunity is also a good idea in many cases. These social innovations part of a social betterment effort, if they are part of the plan from the very beginning. Indeed, many social change efforts focus on creating and/or selling a social innovation. Getting started with social innovations begins with deciding who or what needs to change and how. Then the challenging task of creating, adapting, or combining social innovations begins. Finally, the much tougher job of selling the innovation to your audience begins.

Deciding who or what needs to be changed should come first. The same rule applies whether you want to solve a problem or exploit an opportunity. Tackling a problem that's not a problem to people isn't going to work; you need to focus on educating people first. Chasing an opportunity to do something that doesn't really help people, from their perspective may also be a wasted effort.

Always start with the audience in mind and work backward from there. Maybe you want to combat animal cruelty and neglect in your community. Who will you target with your change efforts? Adult pet owners are the obvious targets, but what about pet stores, property managers, or children? What sort of social innovation seems to be needed? Once you have a target audience in mind it is much easier to focus on an innovation that will work for them. Marketing is also possible, and only effective, when there is a specific audience in mind.

Strategic Application

Some long-range planning is always a good idea. What

resources will you need and when will you need them? For how long do you need them? You might be able to recruit volunteers to work as needed, or you may need to hire freelance graphic designers, writers, or researchers. How much extra money do you need and when will you need it? How will you get the extra money: memberships, grants, donations, or selling cookies at football games? Really, anything that can bring in the required money when its required should be considered.

What is your timeline for achieving your broad goal? You'll need to plan by working backward from that big goal and reaching one milestone at a time. At each stage there will be problems or opportunities that need to be addressed through brainstorming, collaboration, and problem analysis. Will you need any training, advice, books, or software to help here?

The beginning of an effort is a good time to start setting up a creative hit list or a cloud 9(r) file. You'll have a good idea of the problems and opportunities that are coming and can use them to focus peoples' thinking; call it anticipatory problem solving. On a complex initiative your organization/group/coalition may need to set up a concept R&D department. This could be a real group with real meeting space and workspace. More likely, you will want to assemble a team that meets informally, perhaps virtually using Web conferencing tools and teleconferences. They'll need a charter that ties in with the organization's strategic objective.

Professional Help

Sometimes outside consulting and training will be useful. The goal as always is to determine what you need, when you need it, and how you can pay for it. If money is a serious problem you will need to either raise money, work around your area of ignorance, or learn to do things yourself (trading time for money). If the scale of your group or organization makes idea management software a good investment, then you will probably need help with configuring the software. Most brainstorming software for the desktop, and most crowdsourcing applications, are going to be much more user-friendly. Consultants in social marketing or commercial marketing, or structured analysis can be called in for help with challenging problems, or just to provide an outsider's perspective. Formal training on things like lateral thinking or Six Thinking Hats ® or Direct Attention Thinking Tools ® is available and could be helpful, though expensive.

7 – Stealing and Adapting Ideas

The difficulty lies not so much in developing new ideas as in escaping from old ones - John Maynard Keynes

Creative problem solving doesn't always require new ideas. Sometimes the smartest thing to do is to steal a good idea. Creativity can help you spot an idea worth stealing. Creative thinking is probably going to be necessary when you adapt the idea to your circumstances. The world is swimming in ideas for strategies, tactics, products, service, laws, policies, regulations and more. Any enterprising activist, nonprofit employee, or educator should be able to find something that's worth using. The challenge is to find what will work in your situation.

Scientific research has also yielded some potentially practical ideas that could be put to good use by activists, education organizations, governments, and nonprofits. Economics, psychology, and sociology especially offer concepts that have already been adopted by marketers, social workers, counselors, and managers. Why not apply the same social scientific concepts to social betterment?

Marketers and advertisers have ideas worth stealing as well. Marketers and advertisers have to sell things by reaching the right audience with the right message at the right time. Advertisers have to make their messages stick in the viewer's mind. Advertising also competes with other advertising. Obviously, marketers and advertisers have developed a dizzying array of techniques that can, it is hoped, prompt us to go and spend some money. Marketing techniques should be used for social change/social betterment.

Finding Ideas to Steal

First, you need a clearly defined challenge. Generally gathering ideas that may prove useful is also acceptable. Still, it would be better to start off with a specific challenge you intend to address. Why? This will automatically help you focus and will narrow the range of idea sources that need to be searched.

The next step in finding things to steal is defining your information needs. At the simplest level you need to consider whether to look at policies, programs, regulations, services, or products. You need to consider proposals other people have made, and that means you need to know where to look. Don't just look at sources in your own area of expertise; look at other fields. Look for inspiration in sources that have nothing to do with your organization or cause.

Reading things that are far outside your usual areas of interest can also spark new ideas. Try reading different types of magazines or visiting different Web sites. If you've never read a conservative political magazine, go out and buy one. Walk into a bookstore and take whatever is in the top right corner of the first magazine rack you see. Read that magazine (including the ads!) and see if you find anything that can help, even in a modified form.

Read scholarly journals in sociology, management science, organizational research, economics, and psychology. *Administrative Science Quarterly*, journals from the American Management Association, and the American Sociological Association will give you valuable information, If nothing else, you'll learn about books to read and conferences or workshops that are worth attending. Read *Psychology Today, Mother Jones, Mother Earth News, Good, Plenty, Time, Reason*, and *National Review*.

The Internet is also a great place to find ideas worth stealing. Some sites exist mainly to showcases ideas – The Global Ideas Bank at globalideasbank.org is the best known example. Worldchanging.com is another good source of social innovations and technological innovations. Cambrian House, at cambrianhouse.com, is another "idea marketplace" you may want to visit.

Read books outside of your normal field or fields. In particular, read marketing books like *Jumpstart Your Marketing Brain* by Doug Halland *Robin Hood Marketing* by Katya Andreason. If you have an idea to sell directly to people you could read books on social marketing. Read books on advertising too.

Choosing What to Steal

Data, stories, program ideas, policy ideas, innovations, marketing tricks and more can be stolen. You have to attribute information to the source or get permission to use the information (or possibly buy publication rights) in many cases. Aside from that legal caveat, you can borrow, adapt, and use as you see fit. Products, services, legislation, organizations, projects, process improvements, concepts, and systems of technologies and people can all inspire good ideas that suit your own purposes.

Naturally, you want to use scientific research, quotes from scientists, and certain statistics to "sell" your cause. The trick is sometimes to recognize these tidbits when you stumble across them. That's one reason for reading widely and with an eye toward finding material that you can use to advance your cause.

Concepts, general ways of proceeding, could be adapted and applied to a different cause. Almost anything already described in this section is an example of a concept. Internalizing the costs of one's actions is a concept. A specific way of using this concept is to impose a carbon tax on gasoline. Helping people to help themselves is a concept. A specific way of doing this might be to teach some simple psychological tricks to clients of a social service agency who need help controlling their impulses or focusing on a task.

What to Do

The next step in productively stealing ideas depends somewhat on what you took. Statistics and scholarly research have obvious uses in public education, advocacy, program development, fundraising, and policy development. A potential funder will want to see some empirical support for whatever they are being asked to fund. Public education campaigns need statistics to help people understand how serious a problem is, how much they are spending, what sort of risk they are facing and so forth. Activists can make similar use of statistics. Program, project, and policy decisions need to be rooted at least in part on reliable numbers. Those numbers will show where the problem is worst, where the best places are to make an impact with the organization's resources, or where the greatest threat exists. A trend toward increasing teen pregnancy in certain segments of the population will suggest where a project's resources should be directed.

Many social betterment projects seem to start because someone feels that something needs to be done in such-and-such a place. That place is probably one where a problem is highly visible to the person or persons involved in starting the project. This approach is not so bad really. However, taking a more data-driven approach to addressing the same issue or opportunity in a given community will probably give better results, such as more people helped for a given investment of time and energy.

Who Needs What

Different social sector organizations need different tools. Social service organizations need to do qualitative research and quantitative research. Those social service organizations also need to attract clients by publicizing their services and motivating potential clients to take action. Public education organizations need novel ways to get their message out and get people into classes. Business tricks, marketing tricks, and a bit of psychology are all called for. Governments need advertising, marketing, psychology, and sociology. Activists need to use everything, with the specific tool depending on the task at hand. Public education efforts need to be developed with some marketing tricks and psychology, to encourage people to take a desired action. Policy and program ideas need to be founded on research.

Everyone needs to be concerned with finding and adapting ideas to suit a cause or project. Everyone with ideas to sell needs to create ideas based on the characteristics of successful innovations.

What to Use

Each of the major activities that public sector organizations engage in could benefit from using one or more of the techniques in this chapter. Fundraising efforts call for some market research, research on the issue, and some marketing to persuade people that giving is a good idea. Advocacy can only be helped by data on the magnitude of the problem, by applying some psychology, and by using marketing techniques to better get the message out. Any organization can benefit by trying to generate ideas using the business practices listed in Table 4 later in this chapter. Program design can benefit from applying a little psychology, sociology, and economics. Designing a program with the characteristics of successful innovations in mind is going to help.

How to Use Stolen Ideas

Most likely, an idea will be more of an inspiration than an idea you can adopt directly. In the rare cases where an idea is perfect for your organization and community there will still need to be some creativity around marketing the idea once implemented.

Financing might also call for some creative thinking. An idea that's been proven to work in similar circumstances elsewhere might be easier to "sell" to donors and grant making organizations. Novel ideas may need to be creatively financed before grant making organizations and big donors can be recruited.

Advertising and marketing are going to need some creative thinking. This is no different from marketing a novel product or service in a sense. The people with the idea have to show potential buyers (clients, donors, et cetera) why the idea deserves to be supported.

Assuming the stolen idea is like most, it will need some modifications or refinements to work in a new location. A couple of techniques could be applied to the idea to make it work.

Adapting and Combining Innovations

Sometimes the best strategy is to adapt an innovation that's working somewhere else. Adapting these ideas calls for attention to the money, time, skill, and social context in which the adapted innovation will be used. Is there enough time to implement this idea? Is there enough money? Do you know enough about the innovation to estimate a budget? Do you have people with the necessary skills? Can you recruit volunteers or afford to hire someone, perhaps on a temporary basis?

The social context in which you plan to use the innovation is more complicated. Economics, politics, cultural norms, and material culture all influence what can be done and with what level of difficulty. The most relevant factors to consider will depend on what the innovation requires. The social environment has to provide enough resources to make the innovation work. Local laws and regulations need to be consistent with the innovation. Local norms have to make it reasonably easy for people to accept the idea. Using a man wearing a giant condom is not a good way to promote safer sex practices in rural Wyoming!

Two alternatives exist when you set out to combine ideas. One is to simply graft the two ideas together and use them in that form. The other option is to combine ideas and eliminate the disadvantages of each. You can probably find one idea that eliminates a significant weakness in the idea you started working with.

Data Collection

Maybe some first-hand research is called for. Solving a problem or improving society involves learning about the situation in question. People who don't understand the social conditions that shape pregnant teenagers' daily lives can't help those teenagers. A suggestion always sounds better when backed by relevant facts. Sometimes the necessary information exists, and sometimes it has to be collected rather than found. Those are the situations where social research methods are valuable.

Amateur social researchers have several data collection options. The most common and widely used has to be the survey. Everyone's filled out one or two, or so it seems. Everyone thinks it would be easy to create a good survey. While this is partly true, good survey design follows a number of rules. Here are the most important of those rules.

1. Start off with easy and non-threatening questions that will apply to everyone. Doing so will get people relaxed and interested in the survey.

2. Save demographic questions for the end. Ditto for sensitive questions.

3. Don't ask leading questions - "Don't you think nuclear weapons should be banned?"

4. Don't assume your questions are neutral; check them to see if you are unconsciously trying to get a certain answer.

5. Only ask one question at a time. Don't do this: "Do you think the United States should immediately withdraw its troops from Iraq and start serious talks with North Korea?"

6. Be specific. "Do you think the United States government should try to open direct discussions with North Korea on the subject of ending that country's nuclear weapons program?"

7. Don't ask hypothetical questions. Only ask what people are doing or have done.

8. Always follow up in some fashion. Sending an email reminder or a postcard will increase your response rate. The higher the

response rate the more likely your survey responses reflect the true attitudes, behaviors, or beliefs of the people you are studying.

9. Never use convenience sampling if it can be avoided. Always try to get a random sample of people.

Individuals who disagree with those rules should not conduct a survey. Readers will simply not take the survey seriously, except for readers who already share the organization's viewpoint or agenda. Any attempt to hide the questions or sampling strategy will simply lower the survey's credibility even more.

And that list doesn't cover the challenge of figuring out who to survey and how to reach them. You can't use the all-too-common practice of handing out surveys in class or leaving some on the counter at a few local businesses. The people who respond won't necessarily be anything like the general population you want to know about it. If you only care about the students at your university, handing out surveys to a few classes is still a bad idea. The students are likely to differ from the population in unknown ways. Your results won't be valid.

Survey research is still a viable strategy for an organization that depends heavily on numerical data to sell a cause, secure funding, or address a related set of problems. Surveys can also help you better understand your audience, your clients, or your students.

Going out in the field to gather data is another viable technique. Some nonprofits send out volunteers to count birds or collect water samples. The same idea could be extended to most any sort of social change effort. Activists could out and count the number of people visiting city parks with their children. A school could enlist volunteer students to conduct an audit of how the school uses energy. Indeed, the

National Wildlife Federation offers education materials on campus ecology. Campus ecology also concerns water usage, landscaping, waste disposal, food production, and purchasing.

Gathering Qualitative Information

Interview people, do a case study, analyze documents and Web content. All of these techniques can yield valuable *qualitative* information, which is information on the themes and patterns that exist in some research object. Qualitative research can yield a detailed understanding of how people understand a social situation or their social environment. Social scientists sometimes engage in *action research*, a form of qualitative research that involves the research subjects in efforts to change the situation that's being studied.

Interviewing people who have used your organization's services or might do so is a great strategy for learning about your market. Planning should include some data collection anyway. Interviews are a great way to find out what people want, need, or think. You can use the phone or do in-person interviews. In both cases, there is plenty of guidance on interviewing in print and online.

Existing documents, including news items and old case studies, can be part of any planning or evaluation effort. Read and take notes on both what is there and what seems to be missing. Content analysis is the standard approach to learning what those documents contain.

Content analysis is another tool activists, and others, can add to their toolkits. Most people are not going to master action research or content analysis through independent study. Taking a class is going to be necessary for most people.

Qualitative research may provide information that rules out an idea, or suggests an idea. Look out for that sort of information.

Marketing and Promotion

Businesses have developed a dizzying array of promotional and publicity tricks. Anyone who lives in a capitalist country has to be aware of that fact. Anyone interested in changing society or improving some condition needs to think about how those business tactics could be adopted and used.

Some marketing techniques can be used directly and some are suitable as creative-thinking prompts. Here are some marketing tricks and questions:

1. *Vending machines* - "How can vending machines fight climate change?"
2. *Clearance sales* - "What do we need to get rid of?
3. *Sidewalk sales* - "How can a sidewalk sale help reduce teen pregnancy?"
4. *Coupons* - Use humorous fake coupons that publicize your cause.
5. *Buy one, get one free* - What can you combine and "sell"?
6. *Holiday sales* - How can you connect your cause to a Holiday?
7. *Free trials* - How can you help people try out new behaviors?

A nonprofit dedicated to fighting climate change by promoting lifestyle change could use business tricks to promote its cause in several ways. As a creative thinking exercise staff members could reflect on how a sidewalk sale could be used to fight climate change. This is a random input exercise. A sidewalk sale is a good way to, well, sell things or demonstrate things that can reduce or offset carbon dioxide emissions. So, maybe there should be an outdoor Earth Day event featuring books, free tree seedlings, and information on "green" building design.

Businesses and nonprofits form partnerships to sell complementary projects, promote a common cause or to engage in some basic research and development. Sometimes businesses or nonprofits team up with governments. Think like a business owner and look for ways to partner with businesses, nonprofits, and government agencies. Think local – local government, small business and small nonprofits – at first. Find ways to form relationships with national nonprofits that have a similar cause.

Psychology

Persuasion, motivation, commitment-consistency, embedded commands, linguistic bind, presupposition, and cognitive dissonance are psychological tools that the social sector could put to better use. Marketers have used the things that motivate us to sell more of just about everything, from soup to life insurance to vitamins. Psychologists disagree about how the things that motivate or drive human behavior ought to be classified.

An embedded command is simply a few words that are slipped into a sentence, words that issue a command in some way. You could tell people to visit a Web site or call a number or eat less meat without really giving an order.

Cognitive dissonance occurs when something we are doing is in conflict with something we think is right or desirable. Cognitive dissonance can also occur when we become aware that one belief or attitude contradicts another, but that first definition is most often used. Point out that people want to be healthier and save money but spend money on expensive, potentially dangerous synthetic chemicals. Read ads for organic cleaners and milk-based paint. Cognitive dissonance may well be used in one of the ads you read.

A presupposition is an assumption that's embedded in another statement. Assume that people want to save money, make their indoor air cleaner, or clean up the neighborhood. Readers may be motivated to accept whatever you write that seems to follow from that unstated assumption.

A Linguistic bind connects an obvious statement with a desired action. People who agree with the obvious statement may feel compelled to take the desired action. Remind readers that saving energy saves money and you want to stop throwing away money.

Reframing is the process of changing a reader's perception about an issue, problem, behavior, policy, service, product, or program. Environmentalists are increasingly "selling" green technologies and policies using money or health as motivators. They are changing our perception of an issue to one of preserving health or cutting costs.

Commitment-consistency is a technique for getting people to do something that's consistent with the "yes" answer they presumably gave to an earlier question. The question needs to be phrased in such a way that most anyone would answer affirmatively. "Do you want to save 40% or more on your home heating bill?" Readers who are interested in saving money can later be asked to schedule a home energy audit, order a free booklet, or visit an informational page (not a donation page!) on the organization's Web site.

Fund-raising appeals, social marketing efforts, and advertising by nonprofits should tap into one or more of those motivators. Note that this has to be an explicit part of strategy; vague attempts to appeal to emotions, values, or fears will not necessarily work. Sometimes government agencies and nonprofits may tap into a few of those motivators, though this might not be part of a conscious strategy to reach people by pushing their psychological buttons.

Sociology

Sociology is the science of human social organization, from intimate personal relationships to the interactions between cultures. Knowing the social conditions and trends that affect those we want to reach with a message can only help. Crafting good programs, policies, social services, public education campaigns, and social marketing initiatives calls for understanding why people live a certain way. Understanding some of why things are as they are can also help. A little more explanation and a couple of concrete examples will show how a basic knowledge of sociology can support social change and social betterment.

Almost everything that exists in a society has a function, for some part of society. The functions may be trivial in value, or of central importance to the society's survival. The functions may also be intended or not intended. In education, the intended function is to impart certain information that's deemed important to the students. An unintended function may be preparation for highly regimented factory work. This function of education may no longer be valuable in a post-industrial society, but the highly regimented model persists. Prisons exist to punish criminals, but inmates may make new connections and learn new tricks. An unintended consequence of imprisonment is to produce better criminals. Beliefs have functions too, but the functions may not be the same for everyone in the society. Certain religious beliefs may make people easier for the ruling class to control. So, the function of religion may be to provide spiritual guidance and comfort for the masses. For the ruling class, religion may be a social control mechanism. This exact criticism of religion has been expressed many times over the years.

A sociological perspective can help people see the "big picture" of social life. People learn to see events in their lives as part of a larger pattern in society, not just as things that happened to them. Seeing a particular type of event, such as losing another low-wage job, as part of a destructive social phenomenon and not as a personal misfortune raises a person's consciousness. People see the positive and negative patterns in society and may be open to suggestions about how to address those negative patterns.

Many sociologists are interested in the power relations that shape society. It doesn't take an advanced degree to understand that some groups have more power than other groups. Those power differences are not necessarily related to size, intelligence, or individual achievement. History, geography, chance, law, beliefs, and cultural norms all trump personal merit when it comes to determining how a group fares in the distribution of power in a society. All of the same observations apply to wealth as well. Wealth is not distributed in a perfectly equitable fashion; wealth does not depend solely on one's own efforts at making money. Those insights about power and money could be applied to social betterment in many ways.

All communities and groups have certain rules (norms) about how people should conduct themselves. As members of a group or a society we may not think too much about norms. We simply go about our business. Nevertheless, those norms are operating on us and guiding our reactions to new ideas, attitudes, and behaviors. Selling an idea to a group of people will require some understanding of how people think they should act.

Beliefs, laws, schools, economic policies and all other social activities and institutions all have certain functions. That shouldn't be news to anyone. What might be new is the idea that there are manifest functions and latent functions. Manifest functions are planned, as in the curriculum taught in schools. A latent function is something that just happens as the social institution operates. Schools teach people certain habits that will supposedly be useful later in life. Advertising has the manifest function of selling products and services. The latent function may be to create a certain standard for style or consumption habits. Advertising gives us ideas about what a successful person should have or the services he or she should use.

Selling ideas can be easier if you have *valid* and *authoritative* data to share with people. Valid statistics have a logical relationship to the subject and also suggest the sort of relationship that you believe exists. The best way to find valid statistics is to collect them yourself. It will often be more realistic to look for statistics from a trustworthy source. Crime statistics supplied by the police might not be valid, because the police can only tabulate crimes that they know about. While you might have to use police reports, random surveys of citizens will give a better picture of a community's crime rates.

Authoritative statistics come from a reputable source. Demographic data from the United States Bureau of the Census and economic development statistics from the United Nations can be trusted. Data from an unnamed research institute are not helpful. Resist the urge to use terms like 'prominent scholars", "experts", or "research."

That suggestion about not using vague terms to source your data leads into the subject of abusing statistics. The ways we can be misled, intentionally or not, are legion. Charts and graphs can be manipulated to make a trend look more or less pronounced than it really is. You can use one type of "Average" when another is more appropriate. It is easy to find numbers that support a point of view while deliberately ignoring contradictory data. You may want to read the modern-day classic *How to Lie with Statistics* to learn more about "statistics abuse." Don't do those things! Try to catch your opponents doing them, whether on purpose or out of ignorance.

Organizations need to be considered legitimate, or else why would people do business with them, happily obey laws, or willingly donate money? Legitimacy is another sociological concept that might be useful in activism, program planning, and policy. What rules, especially unwritten rules, must an idea adhere to for people to take it seriously? These rules should be collected and written down. The rules can be useful in deciding what counts as a good idea.

Diffusion of Innovations Research

Social scientists have studied what makes certain innovation last, while others fade into insignificance rather quickly, or disappear altogether. Anyone interested in social change or social innovation needs to know what characterizes successful innovations. With this knowledge to draw on the odds of a new idea selling will go up. Successful innovations tend to share certain characteristics. It is easy to understand what the characteristics and how to employ them:

1. *Compatibility* - Show how the idea fits with the audience's

values, economic situation, and needs

2. *Complexity* - Create a simpler version of the idea.

3. *Observability* - Stage a test or demonstration. Conduct a thought experiment and write about that.

4. *Relative Advantage* - Quantify, if possible, and promote the economic and psychological benefits.

5. *Trialability* - Offer a free trail. Break the process into easier steps.

The case of a nonprofit working to promote wider use of solar photovoltaic cells technologies will illustrate how the five characteristics can yield specific ideas.   The ultimate goal is to get people to get more of their electricity for solar cells. Show people how they can save money and reduce *short-term* threats to their family's health. Use hard data to provide a degree of observability – people can see the results of the idea instead of reading fuzzy claims. Encouraging people to buy electricity from a company that sells energy from renewable sources could enhance trialability. People who go along may be receptive to messages about using solar power to get some of their home's electricity.

Consider a regional effort to get people adopt solar power to some degree. Online calculators could help reduce the complexity of adopting solar cells. The calculators can help people determine how many panels of a given size they need, and calculate how much to spend. The same section of the Web site could have a calculator that can give estimated cost savings. The page could also offer information on equipment vendors, installers, and tax incentives. The nonprofit could enhance their idea's *observability* by putting solar cells on a volunteer's home and advertising the monthly and annual energy savings.

Getting Professional Help

Training and consulting are available. Consulting help or professional training will be necessary for some research projects. Evaluation research and hard-core number crunching are the two most common types of research that call for experts. Many survey companies will allow clients to add questions to an existing survey instrument, or they could simply be hired to create and administer a survey. Consider how to share resources with another nonprofit, to cut the costs of getting expert research help.

How would organizations share resources to work on a survey project? Look for one or two other organizations with similar interests or related goals. Talk about what could be accomplished by collaborating on a survey project. Talk about the resources each group can contribute to the project. Obviously, money needs to be involved. People with computer skills, for creating a survey form and entering the data, will be required. The research partners will need to conduct the survey by Web, phone, mail, email, or with in-person interviews.

Classes are always available. Earning a master's degree in statistics may be overkill for most nonprofit workers. Still, taking a class on common statistical procedures or a class on survey research can be a big help. Organizations with a data based approach to operations and planning need to have access to people who can gather and analyze data in different ways. You can find information on training opportunities in the For Further Information section at the end of this chapter.

8 – Design Thinking

Many socially conscious people want to create new programs, policies, systems, and technologies. People want to make the world better, or advance a certain worldview, or get people to change their behavior. New social institutions and technologies have to be designed. *Design* is simply the process of combining technologies, materials, and or processes to deliver a value or values.

Peoples' needs, wants, values have to be accounted for in designs. Our resources, mostly time and money need to be accounted for in a good design. The political climate, the local culture, and the economy are also important. A design that simply advances some ideology is worthless. The design may advance some ideological perspective in addition to delivering other, more practical benefits to users. This chapter is about designing social innovations that deliver value to the user while also making some meaningful change in the world.

In the social sector any system for delivering some benefit to people could be designed or redesigned. Here are some concrete examples:

1. A system for delivering food stamps or similar to eligible families.
2. A policy to control urban air pollution.
3. An after school program to teach high-school students about money management.

Objectives

A design does not need to be original. The design only needs to be original in its application. In fact it sometimes makes better sense to borrow a good design than to invent something entirely new. Regardless of whether the designs are new or simply borrowed and adapted the same basic principles will apply. Some redesign is likely to precede actual use of the design.

We design economic policies, environmental policies, and social policies. The policy's creators must identify the interests, needs, and values of those affected by the policy. Legislators also have needs, interests, and values. Voters on the policy, regulators who will enforce the policy and write specific rules also need to be considered. How can the policy be made more palatable to people? How can this be done in a way that still delivers value?

Social services and social programs are designed or redesigned. A program always has a goal, sometimes quantitative and sometimes qualitative. In both cases we want the program to deliver value of some sort to some group or groups. What are their interests, needs, and values? How can a program be designed for those people? How can the program be designed to account for the cultural, economic, and political climate? What elements of the social environment are critical to success or to *avoiding failure*? What elements of the social environment could be leveraged to improve the service or program?

Social innovations also need to be created with interests, needs, and values. People certainly can't be expected to use a new innovation if they get no value. Sometimes activists forget that their "innovative" ideas have to provide some benefit that people care about. Not "should" care about, but actually care about. Following a formal design process for policies, programs and social innovations will force users to become more "user-focused" and less "self-focused."

Designing policies, programs, and social innovations can always be improved by conducting an environmental scan. Regular content analysis and environmental scanning will also improve designs and redesigns.

Wants, Needs, and Design

Distinguishing between your audience's wants and needs is not useful. People rarely draw any firm distinction between wants and needs. Designs must satisfy wants and needs to be successful designs. Concentrate on wants and needs that relate most directly to a given design. A new education program could appeal to potential students' need for status, but maybe this isn't the most relevant psychological motivator. Start the design process by identifying what wants and needs a design can reasonably be expected to satisfy. Do all of the wants and needs have to be considered? Maybe the design needs to focus on only one or two to be a successful design. Add those to the design brief, the list of required features and performance characteristics.

How would one create a design brief for a social innovation, social program, education program, or policy? See the section below labeled "Design Values" and start there. he answers can be reduced to a list of requirements for the new design. The brief could also contain a list of desired features. Begin the brief with a short statement on the type of design being described and describing the general purpose of the design. A design brief for a program to create business opportunities in a rural part of Africa may begin as follows:

Type of Design - Entrepreneurship program:

General Purpose: To provide a model of financing, marketing help, and mentorship to foster the creation and growth of small businesses in rural Ivory Coast. Emphasis should be on socially- and ecologically-conscious businesses.

Market Research and Design

Who is your design supposed to benefit and how will those people benefit? What do those people want or need? As with conventional marketing, in the selling of social change, it does little good to try and distinguish between a real want and a need. Does Joe *need* a sports car or does he simply want one? These sorts of questions can only be answered by the individual.

Concentrate on what people say they want and need without trying to discriminate between true needs and things that would simply be nice to have. The same rule applies whether you are trying to sell a tangible product, such as vegan frozen entrees, or an idea. The idea of switching to a vegan diet has to seem easy and relatively comfortable. The harder or more uncomfortable the transition the less likely people will go vegan. More than likely, the failure rate will go up among those who do give vegan living a go. People like to try something out before becoming fully committed. It is your responsibility to show them how.

Market research can yield better designs because you will learn more about your audience's habits and personalities. Do they tend to be socially conservative? Are they risk- averse or somewhat adventurous? Are they religious or not? Do you need to target different segments of the population differently? What are the meaningful segments?

You certainly don't know how best to sell your idea unless you know the best ways to reach your audience. Maybe the best "sales" method is the face-to-face meeting. Maybe fliers posted in churches and small businesses would work. Maybe email or printed letters would work. Your own causes and interests will call for reaching other types of people through various media.

Design Values

Providing value through a policy, program, or social innovation is not necessarily easy. Asking many questions related to the values and how they will be delivered and to what group can help. A systematic approach to the design process is going to result in better design. What value or values is the design meant to deliver? To who are the values supposed to be delivered; who is supposed to benefit from the design? The following paragraphs draw heavily from Edward De Bono's description of design values in *New Thinking for the New Millennium*.

What *benefits* will this design deliver and to whom. Spend a few minutes to let your mind range far and wide to uncover many benefits, great and small. How *significant* are the benefits likely to be? "Significance" is a decidedly subjective thing but significance still needs to be considered.

The number of people who benefit and the magnitude of the benefit for each person can provide a rough guide for measuring significance. Homeless people could get substance abuse counseling, if they want it, in half the time it used to take. Is that a significant benefit? Your idea could cut by 1/3 the number of people fined for throwing litter from their cars? Is that a significant benefit?

How *broad* are the benefits? While the size of the benefit matters, it is even more important for many people to get a benefit. An idea cannot lead to all of the benefits flowing to one group while another bears all of the cost. Even if rich and powerful people are expected to bear the cost, the idea faces a practical problem. How can wealthy and powerful people be compelled to absorb the full cost of implementing some idea and getting no significant benefits?

Most any social innovation will have to satisfy a *key value.* Think of the key value as something that must be satisfied, a necessary prerequisite to the innovation being accepted. A key value can be almost anything. Key values can differ from one situation to another even though the social innovation is the same. A key value might be biodegradability (a lubricant or solvent), ease of recycling (plastic products), or simplicity (a water purification system for villages in developing countries).

A value is better if it is *robust.* Values should be delivered in a range of situations and not just under ideal conditions. A solar photovoltaic cell has to deliver a useful amount of electricity even on a cloudy, winter day. Maybe this is one of several reasons why solar power hasn't caught on more widely – the available cells aren't quite good enough. A program to help homeless people should be able to function in situations where financial situations vary greatly.

A design is only delivering value if it can be delivered in *time* to make a difference. A brilliant plan to rebuild New Orleans is not very useful four years after rebuilding began. Delivering the same plan one month after the storm would have been much more useful. Some experts and some environmentalists predicted a Katrina-like disaster, so perhaps such a plan could have been prepared ahead of time.

Speaking of time – if people have to invest a significant amount of time in something, they are less likely to do it. Preparing fresh organic meals every day is nice. The time investment to find a variety of organic ingredients and prepare meals from them is higher than most people are willing to make. The benefit of improved health for people and the environment will not be delivered as well as with another idea. A better idea would be one that is more sensitive to peoples' schedules.

Low cost is an obvious value, or it should be. How many suggestions by activists and social reformers are made with no consideration of the cost, or the benefits relative to the cost? Low cost is a relative value. Upgrading a home to cut energy use by 75% and water use by 50% may cost several thousand dollars, if the homeowners do some of the work themselves. How much will it cost to tear down the house and build a very efficient new house?

The *cost-benefit ratio* is also worth considering. The ability to get as much as possible for a given amount of money or labor is a value. Will your design deliver an adequate performance for the money and time required? Consider what the people who are supposed to use the design (or to pay for it!) will think about the cost-benefit ratio. Does the idea still seem like a good idea? How could the idea be modified to improve the cost-benefit ratio?

Thinking about cost-benefit rations is anathema to many of the socially conscious. Some activists and other social reformers think it is wrong to talk about cost efficiency when we are talking about peoples' lives. This idea is illogical because the more people you help with a given investment of time and money the more good you are doing. Of course, cost-benefit calculations have to consider who is benefiting and how much each person benefits could also be considered. The money it takes to help one drug-addicted homeless man on his fit could buy thousands of sandwiches. But which result is a better use of limited time and money?

Simplicity is a value for three reasons. The fewer things there are to go wrong with the design the better. Likewise, the fewer ways that something will go catastrophically wrong, the less often it will happen. The time element mentioned previously is also an aspect of simplicity (versus complexity). A regimen of 15 pills a day may be able to cure a person of alcoholism, but what if a mistake could kill one of the patients? Maybe a regimen of 4 pills is a better idea, even if the success rate will be lower. People are busy, or think they are. The harder it is to use your innovation the more chances for mistakes.

All designs *involve* people, so the potential users need to be considered in ways above and beyond the ways mentioned previously in this section. Are the benefits of the design easy to understand? If not, then the benefits must be explained. It is not the public's responsibility to figure out the benefits, or to trust that the promised benefits will really be delivered. The innovator has to give an explanation that is both credible and easy to follow. Most people dislike or fear change, so this reality has to be accounted for in any design. Failure to try and overcome the intended users' change resistance is the often going to be critical to the design's success.

Any innovation should be *compatible* with the existing social system, or at least whatever part of the social system the innovation fits into. Current habits, technologies, and social institutions need to be considered in thinking about compatibility. The rules that people use, the technologies they use, and the expectations they have are all relevant whatever we may think about unfair or ecologically destructive patterns that exist.

Small changes are always better, or at least almost always. Innovations are more likely to diffuse successfully if they can be tried out and abandoned easily if some problem appears. Getting people to buy compact fluorescent light bulbs is easier than getting them to buy radically new "green" homes full of unfamiliar technologies and design elements. Perhaps the goal of selling people on "green" homes could be broken down into stages: we try to make compact fluorescent bulbs the norm, then solar hot water heaters, then recycled wood flooring and so on. As Edward De Bono points out in *New Thinking or the New Millennium*, a small change does not have to be a trivial change. The trick is to find small change that will produce maximum value for people.

Negative values, Edward De Bono's term for negative consequences, must also be considered. What could go wrong? What problems will likely follow from wide use of the design? If the problems are significant the design is not viable. Even if people could be tricked into accepting a design with some serious, hidden defect this sort of "sales job" would be unethical and socially destructive. People will quickly discover that organic food is much more expensive. An underhanded attempt to sell people on organic food in spite of known, significant problems with the idea will fail. People will also be very suspicious of any more ideas that come from that group or organization.

A design has to be *realistic*. What counts as realistic is not as easy to define as one might think. Consider whether people with real tastes, budgets, and preferences would actually use the design, or innovation. The easier it is to see the idea fitting into peoples' real lives the more realistic is the design. No matter how good the idea might be in the abstract if it doesn't fare well in that little thought experiment then the idea is not going to be implemented, at least not very widely.

A design should also *work* in the sense of doing what it is supposed to do. The more technical the innovation the more difficult it can be to decide whether the idea is workable or not. This observation applies to technical innovations and to social innovations. A new idea that won't do what was intended by way of changing perceptions or behaviors is certainly not a good idea.

Consider *responsibility* for implementing the design. Do this before the completed design is offered to the public. Someone needs to take responsibility for doing whatever needs to be done to make the design work. All of these design values and the design operations need to be applied to what one hope are off-the-cuff proposals that various activists and social reformers offer on television, on the radio, or in print.

A design could take account of *implementation* as a value. What steps or stages are there in the implementation process? Can you anticipate any obstacles at any stage? Can a big and complex design be broken into segments that are easier or less risky? That last question comes from one of the key characteristics affecting the success of an innovation – trialability. An idea that is easy to implement is more likely to take off.

Design Values and Social Betterment

Social innovations need to take account of many of the preceding values. But, designs meant specifically to change society in some way or improve society require some special considerations. That previous list of design values needs to be supplemented by a few new values. As with the general list of values, this list may not be complete and may not apply in its entirety to any particular design challenge.

Equity - Equity is always a value worth considering when developing a social innovation. People who benefit should bear most of the burden for implementing the idea. Exceptions can be made in the case of the very poor and people who are physically or mentally incapacitated. Refugees are also in a relatively helpless position.

Risk - Voluntary risks, if any risks have to be accepted, are always to be preferred. If there is a risk involved in using the innovation, those who are supposed to use the innovation need to be informed. How will you assess the risk and communicate this risk effectively? The onus here is on the innovator to communicate effectively and not on the public to figure out what could go wrong. Social justice is an easily overlooked value in the design of social innovations.

Equality - A social innovation should not increase social differences in political or economic power. Neither should all of the benefits flow to any group, even the poor, while all of the costs are borne by another group, typically the rich. Why? The well off will see an innovation's downside fight back. Many of the "rich" are simply people who worked hard for many years to attain a very high standard of living. Trying to soak those people because they have "unfairly" accumulated wealth and power is simply not rational.

Design Operations

Brainstorming methods have to be modified in several ways to design a new program, product, service, or policy or social innovation. As De Bono notes in *New Thinking for the New Millennium*, design thinking still requires analysis and judgment. Designers still need to break a subject into component parts and to compare a design against another design or simply compare the idea against a set of criteria.

The subject of design thinking always needs to be defined precisely. It should be possible to tell without a doubt if the design has met the objectives. The objective could be broad: "We need to encourage use of wind power to grow at double the present rate." A narrower objective would also work well. A nonprofit manager may decide to create a new program that will increase the graduation rate of program participants from 75% to 90%.

Be able to move fluidly between concepts and specific ideas and back up to concepts is important to successful design. The first design operation, moving up from an idea to a general concept, enables to extract the general direction you want to go as you create a design. The ability to move from a concept to a new idea is the ability to create new, possibly better, ways of using a concept.

Design thinking involves being able to look for alternatives. How else can we create a policy that will achieve our goal? What other idea could we sell? Similarly, design calls for challenging the current way of doing things. "Is this the only way to teach kids about the dangers of unprotected sex?" "Is regulation the best way to curb water pollution?"

Good designs need to account for more than just technical or financial considerations. Time, culture, average incomes, laws, regulations, and the natural environment are all very broad factors. Use Consider All Factors to make sure the specific factors that affect a design are considered.

Maybe an existing idea is the subject of design. The idea will, by definition, need to be changed in some way. No design would be required if you just used an existing idea. An existing idea may need a dramatic *change* or the idea may need to be *modified* in one or two small ways. How can the existing idea (design) be improved? Using one of Michael Michalko's brainstorming tools – SCAMPER – should help. Chapter 8 contains details on using SCAMPER. An idea can also be developed in the sense of building on strengths and reducing weaknesses by using SCAMPER.

Even if the idea is not very practical as originally conceived, there might be one or two features that can be used. Take one of the features and see what can be done with it. Could that feature be a workable idea? Maybe the feature leads to a concept that can be put into practice using a different idea. The idea becomes a potentially useful design.

Use provocations to find new ideas or to improve an existing idea. Stepping stone, escape, and wishful thinking can all be helpful.

Many initial designs will need to be strengthened in some way. Most any design could be strengthened in some way. Use Pros-Cons-Fixes to identify and correct weak points in the design.

A design effort may call for analyzing the existing approaches, designs, technologies, or institutions to see how they work. Analysis may reveal the best way to subdivide a project into component parts. Each component could be dealt with separately.

Complex design tasks can be divided into parts, each of which can be attacked individually. The parts in question have to be defined for the particular project. A program might be divided into recruiting, teaching, and retaining students. Or, the program could be divided up into recruitment, lesson plans, presentations, and learning activities. A program of substance abuse counseling could be divided into recruitment, intervention strategy, and retention strategy.

Using another brainstorming technique, random input, can reveal the seeds of a good design. Random input is useful both when a radically new idea is desired and when a breakthrough in thinking about some issue is required. Maybe we need a better way to discourage middle school students from trying drugs.

Design Brief for an Environmental Education Program:

This is a program intended to teach people about the benefits of using "green" technologies when they remodel or restore a home. The focus will be on homeowners rather than on contractors or home improvement store managers. What would the designers of an innovative new program for this audience need to consider? It will be helpful to consider the design requirements one category at a time.

Cultural Environment – People are thrifty and individualistic, with certain widely shared ideas about home design and aesthetics. Savings, style, price, and comfort are likely to be major considerations when selected designs or materials.

Political Considerations – There are probably grants or loan programs that people can apply for just to support "green" remodeling efforts.

Legal Considerations – The program needs to account for local building regulations, licensing requirements, and any historic preservation laws. Blithely suggesting something that violates local laws will get us nowhere.

Economic Considerations – The design may need to account for interest rate changes, average income of homeowners, budgets for most remodeling projects, budget for most renovation projects, local sources of green materials and green energy, and local sources of recycling materials. Local income matters as well. Cool new technologies are worthless if people can't afford them.

Technological Considerations – Levels of Internet access should influence our means of disseminating information. The cost-benefit ratio of "mature" green technologies will also need to be considered.

Design Values – Generally, the design must account for the preceding facts about the social environment and it must be realistic given the organization's staff and financial resources.

****

Designing Social Innovations

Almost any new way of doing things can be a social innovation, as long as technology is not the main part of the innovation. A new way of connecting people using a Web site would still be a social innovation. A new programming language is not a social innovation. New jobs, job functions, laws, nonprofit programs, organizations, policies, procedures, regulations, and social institutions are all examples of areas where social innovation is possible and desirable. A new way of dividing up household work among children in a household may be innovative but is not a social innovation.

Many good examples of social innovations already exist. Maybe you just need to find one and adapt it to your organization or community. Edward De Bono once suggested that the water intake pipes for factories be downstream from the water outlet pipes. Factory owners would be motivated to keep the water clean. Another of his suggestions was that people should be allowed to park their cars for as long as they wish, provided the headlights are left on.

Social Betterment Goals

Activists, nonprofit staff, and some government staff are concerned with alleviating social problems or with exploiting opportunities to make society better in some way. Social betterment goals can be reached more efficiently if some design thinking is applied to them. Programs can reach more people or with a higher success rate. Education campaigns will teach more people something. Policies will have a greater effect on the targeted behavior. Advocacy efforts will have a greater impact on the public.

Schools need new policies, new rules, new after-school programs, and new recruitment strategies. Teachers need new teaching tools, new exercises for students, and new ideas for using technology. Meeting those education needs with new designs, or old designs adapted to new circumstances, requires design thinking. The designs naturally must fit with the norms, regulations and traditions of the schools. Adult education designs must met the needs and tastes of potential students. Public education campaigns need to be designed to present their lessons in ways that will be agreeable to the audience.

Activists, nonprofit managers and (sometimes) government officials want or need new ways to serve constituents and clients. Maybe a design needs to target people who could benefit from a service, if they used the service. Designing new programs for the homeless, at-risk youth, watershed protection and dozens of other social goals will call for analysis, creative thinking, and some salesmanship. Equity is naturally going to be an n important consideration in social programs.

Governments make policy, companies, professional associations, school systems, university faculty, religious leaders, and activists try to influence policy. Those policies influence our businesses, finances, jobs, health, and educational opportunities. On a grander scale, policies influence national security, economic growth, and environmental quality to name a few areas of influence. New public policies are always "designed" in an ad hoc fashion.

What is needed is willingness by those who make policy, or influence policy, or want to influence policy to use design thinking. Taking time to explore the true nature of issues to be addressed by a policy would also be time well spent. Brainstorming, decision analysis, potential problem analysis, situation analysis and lateral thinking tools can complement design thinking. What are our priorities in this situation? A lateral thinking tool called First Important Priorities can help clarify priorities.

And what happens to an idea for a new policy? Partly, the fate of an idea is determined by the influence of the person or group presenting an idea and partly by the political climate. A liberal idea is unlikely to make it through a Republican-dominated Congress.

9 – Brainstorming

Brainstorming is a simple process of sitting down, alone or with a group, and coming up with some ideas. The process is pretty much the same regardless of whether you are brainstorming new product ideas, new marketing tricks, or new social service programs. That's probably what most people think of brainstorming.

That simple definition of brainstorming is accurate, but incomplete. Other factors in idea generation need to be considered too. What counts as a good idea? How do you evaluate your ideas against those criteria? It is extremely unlikely that brainstorming will produce a ready-to-use idea. A good idea will most likely need some refinement. You can use simple techniques to help with establishing evaluation criteria, generating ideas, evaluating ideas, and refining ideas. As you'll see, these techniques will pay off in better ideas.

This chapter begins with an examination of how we can decide what counts as a good idea. Then you'll learn several brainstorming techniques. Finally, you'll learn how to apply these techniques to challenges that are common to governments, nonprofits, and schools. Along the way you'll also learn how to get professional help. The "Recommended Reading" section lists several books on creative thinking.

Exploring Your Challenge

Before starting to address a problem or exploit an opportunity some exploration of the issues is in order. Specifically, people need to consider why they are addressing the challenge in question. A technique for exploring a challenge simply involves asking "Why?" several times. The point of those questions is to get at your real reasons for working on a challenge. An activist may ask why he should work on reducing fossil fuel consumption in the United States. The answer, "to combat global climate change,' leads to another question: "Why do I want to combat global climate change?" A likely answer here is that because global climate change is the biggest environmental threat confronting civilization. So, why focus on the United States? Maybe there is no good reason. Maybe the United States is a good subject because of our enormous energy consumption. The United States also has unmatched scientific and technical prowess to bring to bear on the technologies we need to fight climate change.

Another set of questions can help to better define how to address a challenge. Asking questions will yield a deeper understanding of the challenge. Ask these questions:

1. Who – Who should work on this challenge?
2. What – What should we focus on? What is the objective here?
3. Where – Where (group or geographic area) should we focus our efforts?
4. Why – Why do we care about this challenge?
5. When – When can we/should we take action?
6. How – How can we make the most impact give available resources?

Author Michael Michalko encourages readers to think more broadly about addressing a challenge by asking a question that begins "In what ways might I..." and seeing where that answer leads. Returning to the fossil fuels example, someone would ask: "In what ways might I work to reduce fossil fuel use in the United States?"

Another of Michalko's suggestions is that people consider the personal benefits they can expect from addressing that particular challenge. Will the rewards, financial or otherwise, be enough to compensate for the effort and stress involved? Check that conclusion before proceeding. Maybe the challenge can be attacked in a way that will be more personally rewarding. Maybe someone else can be recruited to take on the challenge. Different people evaluate efforts and rewards differently. Or, maybe the other person would find it easier to make things happen.

Easy Brainstorming Tricks

The easiest tool to use is one that resembles conventional brainstorming. You decide on a specific "creative focus" and spend three minutes generating as many ideas as possible. For example, you could decide on the creative focus "Attract more students to my non-profit's financial planning classes." Then you spend a few minutes concentrating on ways to attract more students. At this stage there is no need to worry about practicality.

Challenging the status quo, another technique created by Edward De Bono, requires you to question assumptions, objectives, and standard operating procedures. Rules, processes, and procedures are also subject to challenges. That isn't to say anyone should do anything confrontational or dangerous or start a fight. We just need to challenge the need or those rules, assumptions, objectives and so forth to see if any realistic ideas emerge.   Standard procedures are always ripe for challenges. Sure, the standard procedures may be quite good, but they could probably be improved in some way. The standard way to get students in your classes may be to advertise in various newspapers, publicize your Web site, and run ads in one or two national magazines. Maybe you should focus on free community newspapers instead of the larger-circulation newspapers. Maybe a "standard" sort of class needs to be replaced or updated in some way.

Maybe your objectives aren't the right ones given your resources. Maybe the issue you want to work on should be addressed by pursuing other objectives. Financial planning may need to be broken down into subtopics that you can teach in print, using newsletters or the Internet. Maybe you need to look at other ways to help people be more fiscally responsible. Fiscal responsibility may not be as much of an issue as smart shopping.

Random input is a surprisingly powerful but simple technique for generating ideas. You can read about several variations of this technique. The variations all involve stating a challenge and comparing it to some randomly selected word, phrase, object, activity, or photograph. You generate associations, features, or characteristics of that random stimulus. Then you look for connections between each item on your list and the challenge in question.

You may be interested in helping homeless people get their lives back together. Conventional methods don't appeal for whatever reason. So, you decide to look for a big, new idea using the random input technique. Opening a dictionary at random you see that the first noun listed is "lizard." Lizards are cold-blooded. They have scales. Most lizards are carnivores. Boys like to catch lizards. Some people like to keep lizards as pets. Lizards are like little dinosaurs.

Be sure that the random input you pick is not related somehow to your challenge. In that homelessness example, "shelter" would be a poor choice. Using photographs for random input would mean avoiding a soup kitchen or anything else associated with homelessness. If that word came up you could simply turn the dictionary to another page and take the first noun on that page. It is important to not go looking for a word that sparks ideas. You may not be able to break out of your habitual way of thinking – and this is the reason for using random input – resulting in ideas that are neither particularly inventive nor especially valuable.

Forcing connections between a challenge and something seemingly very different can produce powerful ideas. Battling homelessness is like bass fishing. Bass fishing involves learning the habits of bass, buying a rod and reel, finding a likely spot to fish, and selecting the right lure or live bait. Do any of those characteristics of bass fishing suggest a new approach to battling homelessness? That list of characteristics suggests this tactic: Study what will motivate homeless people to enroll in a training program and stick with it. You should stay away from activities or processes that are something like your challenge. Don't compare battling homelessness to running a soup kitchen.

****

Random Input: Activities

Pick something from this list and try to force connections between the characteristics of the activity or and your challenge. Make it random by selecting a column based on the month when you were born, then use the first thing in that list. Alternately, roll a six-sided die and use the corresponding concept.

Die Roll	January – March	April – June	July – September	October – December
1	Buying a car	Hosting a dinner party	Running a marathon	Planning a wedding
2	Growing a garden	Mowing the lawn	Buying a bicycle	Cutting your own hair
3	Piloting an airplane	Planning a vacation	Grocery shopping	Learning to dance
4	Planning a date night	Buying Christmas gifts	Painting a house	Throwing a birthday party
5	Going on a diet	Riding a horse	Learning a language	Buying a house
6	Cleaning your closets	Planning a garage sale	Looking for a job	Planning for retirement

****

Generating ideas is not the same as generating good ideas. And what counts as a good idea depends on your circumstances. Consider these factors when you are thinking about what counts as a good idea:

1. Time   How much time do you have?
2. Talent – What skills do you have access to?
3. Money – How much can you afford to spend?
4. Legality – What will local laws and regulations allow?
5. Connections – Do you know the right people to implement this idea?

6.   Norms – Will local cultural standards allow for your idea to take hold?

Provocation is one of Edward De Bono's many thinking tools. A provocation forces us out of our normal patterns of thought. The usual form of provocation is really a form of random input. Or, you can make a truly nonsensical statement and see where it leads. "Po homeless people eat air." This is obviously absurd but thinking about how people could live on air may lead you to a novel way of helping homeless people.

De Bono lists other types of provocations. Moment-to-moment provocation involves envisioning the idea being put to use and imagining what would happen.   The escape provocation reverses or eliminates a certain assumption so that we can look for practical new ideas. Wishful thinking provocations are just that – fantasies about what would happen if…industry actually cleaned the air, people could live without food. Substitute any "Wouldn't it be nice if…" statement that fits with your cause or goal. What practical way of moving toward that fantasy can you identify?

Systematic Idea Generation

Some brainstorming techniques are systematic ways of teasing out new ideas, as opposed to the conventionally "creative" approaches outlined above. Three relatively easy techniques will increase your ability to generate useful new ideas. Force field analysis is a tool for evaluating the forces affecting a given situation. Morphological analysis is a systematic way of describing the characteristics of a product or service. A concept map (or concept fan) is a way to reveal the concepts behind an approach to a challenge, with the intent to find new ways of carrying out those concepts.

SCAMPER

This is a systematic tool for evaluating ways to deal with a challenge. Each letter stands for an operation that's performed in the process of looking for new ideas. SCAMPER is an acronym for Substitute, Combine, Adapt, Magnify or Modify, Put to Other Uses, Eliminate, and Rearrange. Try asking the following questions adapted from *Thinkertoys* by Michael Michalko:

- *Substitute* – What can be substituted? Who else can do what we want to do? What location or setting can be used instead?

- *Combine* – Can we combine purposes with another group or project? What technologies can be combined? What social innovations can be combined? With whom, or what group, could we combine resources?

- *Adapt* – What ideas could we incorporate? What process, program, or project could we copy?

- *Magnify or Modify* – What can we exaggerate (to make a point or to attract attention)? What could we do much more of? In what ways might we expand our reach? Our impact? Our public profile? What could be changed to make the idea more attractive or more powerful? In what other way could we present our idea to others? How could we change our idea to make it more attractive?

- *Put to Other Uses* – How else could our idea be used? What concept is being implemented with this idea? Can the concept be acted upon in another way?

- *Eliminate* – What element of the plan or idea could be cut out? Could we do things on a smaller scale?

- *Rearrange* – How else could we organize our project or program? Could we change the order of things? Could we change the schedule? The sequence of events involved in implementing the idea?

Mind Mapping

Mind mapping is really rather easy to learn and use. The basic idea is to draw out a diagram of ideas and concepts and facts, while studying it for new ideas. Here is a basic outline of the method and the principles that apply:

- Use shapes and colors to denote different subtopics.
- Use keywords and phrases only.
- Work outward from the center of a piece of paper wherein you've identified the map's subject.
- Connect major subtopics directly to that central box or bubble.
- Use lines to connect ideas to their respective subtopics..

You can draw lines between ideas or facts that you originally associated with different subtopics. Those novel connections may lead to new ideas or new concepts from which concrete ideas can flow.

Morphological Analysis

You can find ways to change or improve an idea by combining

the elements of your subject in new ways. The "idea box," as author Michael Michalko calls it, is a tool for doing that. A fancier term for the idea box is the morphology box. Morphology refers to the shape of things. A morphology box is used to specify the parameters of a subject and the variations on each parameter. New combinations of the variations on each parameter can yield new ideas.

You begin constructing an idea box by specifying your challenge. Suppose we want to get more people to conserve energy at home. Our challenge could be stated as follows: "In what ways can we convince more people to use energy-conserving technologies at home?" The next step in constructing an idea box is to define the parameters of our challenge. A parameter is simply a characteristic element of the challenge. If the element were missing we would not have a problem or challenge to work on. General examples of parameters include size, material, audience, advertising medium, shape, target market, an price range. You'll probably be able to use one or more of those parameters in thinking about your own challenge. You will probably need to come up with others that are unique to your challenge.

Returning to our energy conservation challenge, we might think of the parameters and variations listed in the table on the next page. A quick review might suggest other options for each column, but this is a good sampling of possibilities.

****

An Idea Box on Promoting Energy Conservation

Audience	Technology	Medium	Scope
Homeowners	Solar PV	Web site	Local
Contractors	Efficient lighting	Direct mail letters	Regional
Developers	Passive solar	Magazine ads	State-wide
Utilities	Wind energy	Radio ads	National
Home renovators	Improved insulation		International

****

The underlined items in the table suggested the possibility of using advertorials (an advertisement that reads like a short essay) to reach professionals and do-it-yourselfers who are remodeling buildings. An organization could use advertorials to publicize two or three facts about the economic and psychological benefits of passive solar design. The advertorials could be published in the business or real estate sections of regional newspapers.

That new public education strategies can you identify in that box? You can probably find something both novel and practical. Maybe the idea will be more realistic for your organization that conventional methods. Maybe the idea will give much better results than conventional approaches. Without going through a formal process of generating ideas, you would never have the chance to find out.

Concept Maps

Sometimes it can help to revisit the concepts you are working with to generate an idea. A concept is simply a general way of doing something. Reducing demand for fossil fuels is a concept. The general direction of your thinking may be to cut fossil fuel use. The concept of reducing fossil fuel use can be carried out in many specific ways. Each specific technique we think of could be an idea, or the technique might be another concept that leads to other ideas.

You create a concept map by working backward from a general direction, to concepts, then to specific ways of carrying out those concepts. This process should yield one or more workable and original ideas. A general direction might be "Triple solar power use in the United States, by 2017." Three concepts that constitute paths toward that general direction might include make it normal, make it easy, and incentivize it. Here are some ideas prompted by each concept:

- *Make it Normal* – run public service ads, perhaps focused on one geographic area, in home and garden television programs; run educational ads in lifestyle magazines
- *Make it Easy* – recruit volunteers to help people select and install equipment; do the same but focus on people who are remodeling their homes; or, focus on investors who buy, renovate, and resell homes; research and advertise the economic benefits
- *Incentivize it* – campaign for tax credits for homeowners who install solar power equipment; campaign to waive the state and local sales tax on the equipment and on installation services.

Are any of those ideas new and practical? I'm not aware of anyone who volunteers to help people select and install solar power equipment. It is not clear that an organization could find the right people, but perhaps that is possible. Perhaps an organization with more resources could recruit and train volunteers. That simple example only contained one layer of concepts. Other concept maps may have two or three layers of concepts. A concept map may also have to be back filled: As you write down ideas, you may discover that an idea represents a new concept. Add that new concept to the concept layer of the map. The new concept may lead to one or two new ideas that may not have occurred to you without working through the concept map.

Using Brainstorming Techniques to Change the World

Brainstorming has many uses. The best tools for each use may differ. You don't try to use a screwdriver for a task that calls for a wrench. You will better results if your creative thinking tools are matched to the nature of your creative challenge. So, the challenge lies in deciding what to use in a given situation. Edward De Bono gives extensive guidance on selecting lateral thinking tools for different situations. In a situation where you are designing something entirely new, random input will help get ideas flowing. Wishful thinking provocations might lead to useful ideas as well. Design can begin with the design thinking guidance given in Chapter X or de Bono suggests that random input can provide a new approach to the subject. Challenging the assumptions and usual ways of approaching the subject can also help.

A few tools from other writers also need some more explaining. When should you use morphological analysis? This technique is mostly used for design or redesign. How else could we deliver this message or this knowledge? How else can we design this item, so it is more environmentally friendly? Concept mapping is good for finding new approaches to a task. Work back to the concept that guides current thinking. Is there another, superior way to carry out the concept? Asking questions is always a good idea when you are investigating a challenge for the first time or when you are trying to decide what counts as a good idea.

Some techniques are applicable to just about any situation. Creative focus, random input, and forced connections could be used with any challenge. Morphological analysis is best used if you want to find a new approach to an existing program, public education effort, or advocacy effort. Morphological analysis could also help you identify new approaches to fundraising. A concept map can help you clarify your thinking about how to approach a challenge by spelling out the concept you are using and (perhaps) revealing another practical way of carrying out the concept. Try using two of more techniques to explore your idea in detail.

Getting Professional Help

You can probably learn enough to use these techniques and refine your ideas without expert help or training. However, many people learn better in a structured environment. This is why classes are a good option for organizations. Besides the structure provided by formal training people might be too busy with their regular work to study and practice brainstorming techniques.

Some situations may call for working with consultants. This is especially true for three situations. Members of an organization may try to be creative, but they are caught in the habits of thought that characterize an organization. Novel ideas can be squashed before they even get worked out in any detail. A consultant can bring a useful outsider's perspective. Working with experts can lend credibility to your organization's efforts. Finally, some problems or challenges can be exceedingly difficult to handle. Getting expert help can make it much easier to come up with a workable idea that's been carefully evaluated and refined. A creative idea is not necessarily better than an uncreative idea. Creativity is only a characteristic, not an evaluation criterion. People sometimes forget that.

Brainstorming Software

Many problem-solving techniques have been programmed into software. The software streamlines the problem-solving process and shortens the learning curve for some of the sophisticated pen-and-paper techniques. Whether the learning curve actually gets any shorter partly depends on the user's comfort level with software. Some people are able to easily jump into learning a new piece of software. Other people avoid learning software. Creative-problem solvers can function effectively without software, but software support can be valuable.

Brainstorming software generally fits into one of four categories. The first category, representing the easiest software to use automates a technique called random input. A brainstorming process called mind mapping is popular and, not surprisingly, several software vendors offer mind mapping software. Comprehensive problem solving software that uses several techniques to generate and evaluate ideas is covered next. Software that's designed to facilitate collaboration on brainstorming is the most complicated type of software and is covered last. You'll also learn the best way to get started with brainstorming software, and how to ramp up your investment in the software.

When Software Makes Sense

Different software works best in different situations. Your comfort with software in general and your budget will largely determine the best place to start. The less computer-savvy may want to start with software that does one thing or just a few. Some brainstorming software is available for free trials. So, findings something that you can try for free would be a good move. The Brainstorming Toolbox® (by Infinite Innovations Ltd.) is a good example, and it also helps users evaluate ideas. Simpler brainstorming software is available from $39 a copy. Some software manufacturers will give a discount for purchasing multiple licenses.

If you've ever created a mind map, or if you are curious about mind mapping several software titles are available. Prices vary from nothing to over $200. Mind mapping is not that difficult. The software isn't truly necessary to create good mind maps, but using mind mapping software does offer two advantages. You can easily share mind maps electronically. Mind mapping software makes it easy to focus on the map's contents rather than on the act of drawing the map.

People who want more support for their problem-solving efforts may want to consider comprehensive software packages. Software like ThoughtOffice(r) and MindSights(r) can help users brainstorm, evaluate ideas, analyze problems, and make better decisions. Both packages include modules for various tasks, including strategy creation, idea generation, marketing, advertising, and design (creating something new or improving something that exists now. These problem solving suites can cost over $700 and come with relative steep learning curves. However, people who want a range of capabilities in their software, or people who deal with especially complex issues may want to spend the extra money.

Word Processors

Perhaps it shouldn't surprise anyone that any word processing program is a good brainstorming tool. It doesn't matter what title you use or how sophisticated a user you happen to be. Most PCs ship with simple text editing software. All you need to do is write down your challenge then take a few minutes to brainstorm ideas. You can edit the list endlessly. You can attach the list to an email message and send it to friends or coworkers. While you're at the computer you could even do some online research and make notes in the same document.

This book contains dozens of questions that could be typed and answered in a document. Answer the SCAMPER questions or the Phoenix questions. Create a document for each set of questions and keep the documents around for when some creativity or critical thinking is called for.

Mind maps, decision-event trees, and concept maps can be created using software like ConceptMap®, ConceptDraw®, and SmartDraw®, (for mind maps).

General Applications

Brainstorming software is potentially useful in all types of organizations. Likewise, software can be used for some tasks that are common across organizations. Design, improvement, and advertising all call for some creativity. Idea generation and evaluation are important for all three tasks. Using brainstorming software makes sense to organize and streamline the process makes sense.

Design tasks such as newsletter design, Web site development, art for products like t-shirts or bumper stickers, and business processes all need to be designed. Social programs of all types also need to be designed unless the organization is just copying an existing program. Even in those situations some brainstorming to adapt or improve the program may be called for. Existing products, services, educational programs, and Web designs may need improving. Of course the same comments apply to pen-and-paper techniques. It is a matter of budget and personal work style whether to use software or pen-and-paper techniques.

Idea Management

Collaborative software is one of the hot topics in IT in early 2007. It should be no surprise that companies have developed collaborative software that supports innovation and invention. Companies like Imaginatik® and OVO® are marketed to companies wanting to manage complex process or campaigns that must build on input from a geographically dispersed population.

Software companies originally created this software for businesses and this is how idea management software is typically marketed. Specifically, idea management software helps people cooperate to generate and evaluate ideas for a particular project, campaign, or other effort. The effort in question doesn't need a defined end point. New ideas for solving management problems might always be welcome.

Idea management software offers several common

features. Most are hosted on the organization's own computers. Jenni and Brightidea.com are two exceptions with their Web-based services that can be used for one "campaign" or rented by the month. In 2007, Brightidea.com's prices began at $1950 a month for 600 users to access the service. That should be enough users for most nonprofits. Idea management is a collaborative effort. The software often has a capability to store ideas separately from the idea generation module. Most software allows a manager to edit and filter ideas, combine ideas, and evaluate ideas.

Nonprofits that have offices in multiple locations or relationships with other organizations in different cities might need idea management software. This is especially true for international organizations and global networks of nonprofits. Idea management software might be used to collaborate on an international issue, such as sustainable development in the Southern Hemisphere or eradicating poverty. The software could be used to organize idea-generating efforts focused on one aspect of such large and complex issues.

****

Nonprofit Applications of Brainstorming Software:

This list offers some likely ways to use brainstorming software for social betterment and related purposes.

1. Creating campus social marketing campaigns.
2. Developing novel publicity stunts, slogans, and demonstrations.

3. Coping creatively with financial challenges.

4. Designing social marketing campaigns focused on a community or segment of the population.

5. Developing new fundraising strategies and tactics.

6. Finding new media or venues in which to promote a cause or idea or advertise a fundraising initiative.

7. Inventing new policies and programs to address social issues.

8. Marketing a social service or nonprofit educational program.

9. Developing a better understanding of the audience for your message.

10 – Evaluating Your Ideas

Coming up with a new idea is only the beginning of the struggle to innovate. Ideas have to be evaluated. Implementation brings risk of outright failure, cost overruns, and negative consequences. Rigorous idea evaluation will reduce but not eliminate risk. Borrowed ideas are no different. In addition, borrowed ideas also need to be adapted to a particular organization's circumstances. This adaptation process raises additional risks of introducing problems into implementation or new and undesirable consequences.

Evaluation can also produce positive, unplanned consequences. Evaluation may reveal something good that needs to be given special attention. Perhaps evaluation reveals a new benefit that would come from implementing the idea. The positive consequence should be acknowledged and built upon. This chapter offers more detail on the process of getting more value of unexpected but desirable consequences. Positive consequences can emerge after and the idea is implemented. Innovators need to pay attention to these happy occurrences and capitalize on them. Use the consequences in advertising. Create a new program designed to help more good things happen.

Culture

Beliefs, lifestyles, norms, physical infrastructure, technology, and values can all influence an idea's reception. Some of the influences are obvious, but not all of them. People sometimes overlook the seemingly obvious and make mistakes.

Beliefs about many different aspects of the world can potentially affect the sale-ability of an idea. Teaching humanist philosophy a "life skills" class would not be accepted in many parts of the United States, due to our Christian heritage. Beliefs about gender roles can shape an audience's response. Many people still fill that certain things are for men and certain things are only for women.

An idea must have a decent fit with the lifestyles of those who are supposed to adopt the idea. Maybe an architectural firm needs to specialize in building green mansions and luxury condos.

Norms, the rules society operates by, are going to shape the reception of an idea. In obvious cases the idea will violate some law or regulation that you weren't ware of. In other cases, the idea simply violates some rule of correct conduct that is not written down but is still taken seriously. Other relatively minor rules can stand in the way of an idea. People don't want to look or feel strange.

Social reformers can't overlook the influence of a community's physical infrastructure on whether an idea succeeds or not. Many questions about the infrastructure can be answered easily. Economic development may require answers to questions about utilities: Is the telephone service reliable enough? Is the water safe to drink? Many other questions about the infrastructure would apply to other types of idea. Coming up with the right questions and getting answers may take time and effort but this process is not particularly difficult.

Technology places some obvious limits on what can be accomplished. If 2% of the target population has Internet access then a Web-based education campaign will fail. Existing to be considered and built upon. Plans that focus on experimental technology (or speculative technologies like fusion power) have a very high risk of failure! Stick with proven technologies, unless engineering and invention are part of your organization's work.

Politics

The political climate influences the odds of successfully implementing an idea. An idea that works in a liberal area may not work in a conservative area. It pays to be careful how an idea is presented. In conservative communities advertising sponsorship by the federal government may actually be a mark against your idea in peoples' minds. Similar sentiments will exist in some areas of other countries. In many cases a university or respected nongovernmental organization, particularly a church or an academic research institution is a better choice to advertise. Even if the idea does get government money as well, advertising affiliation with a respected social institution could help the cause.

Time

Is there enough time to mobilize the people needed to put the idea into action? If there is no externally imposed deadline, are the people who need to implement the idea available? Do you have enough people with enough time to implement the idea? If not, can other tasks be dropped entirely or moved down the list of priorities? If neither option is workable then there is always the possibility of recruiting volunteers to work on the idea or take over other tasks so staff can work on the idea. Which tactic makes sense will depend on whether or not the staff has the necessary skills.

An area's economy can affect the prospects for an idea in several ways. The available technology is relevant, as are the dominant industries and the most common skills. Incomes and credit also affect what is realistic. Some countries have underdeveloped or nonexistent credit systems. Some parts of United States are quite poor, by American standards, so credit may not be widely available. All ideas have to be context-specific – an obvious but easily ignored rule. So what if urban agriculture *seems* like a good idea? If people lack the money or credit to start urban farming businesses, then the idea is a nonstarter.

Other Resources

Status and reputation can also work wonders for the credibility of an idea. An organization that's not well known might be able to team up with a more well-known organization or even an individual "champion" for the idea in question.

Most ideas need things. An organization needs the equipment, supplies, and professional services that the idea requires. If these resources aren't in the organization now, then they will have to be acquired somehow. Maybe the funds exist or can be raised through a grant. Soliciting donations may work. Some organizations barter for goods or services. A business or another nonprofit in the area may have just the thing that's needed to help an idea along and a willingness to trade. Considering possible trading partners and approaching one or two can be a smart tactic, stretching the organization's resources will speeding along implementation of the idea.

Final Evaluation Steps

Evaluating ideas doesn't really need to be all that complicated, does it? We usually have a sense of what will work for us given our social environment and resources. A complicated process of idea evaluation isn't always necessary. If you are intimately familiar with the problem, organization, and social environment an intuitive process of evaluation perhaps in discussions with a few coworkers is enough. Of course if the states aren't particularly high you can afford to evaluate ideas in a simplified manner and get on to more important matters.

Say you want to foster more creativity among your staff. You get the idea to provide some resources that will help them get good ideas. The obvious and inexpensive options are to buy some cheap brainstorming software or to buy several copies of a book. This sort of idea doesn't need to be subjected to rigorous analysis; pick whatever option seems reasonable and go with it.

If an idea involves connecting a network of people who share common social betterment goal, then a formal evaluation process is called for. Maybe your specific idea is to purchase idea management software. You want to be very sure that the specific idea/plan you decide to implement is sound. Those sorts of idea are the ideas to which this chapter's tools apply.

Prioritizing

Not all ideas that pass a rigorous examination are automatically usable. Almost all organizations will need to manage their resources, focusing on certain ideas and leaving others behind. This same logic applies across the many activities in any organization and to the ideas generated in response to a particular problem. Using one of three simple decision analysis tools can make the selection process a little easier.

Michael Michalko introduces a technique called "Worrywillie's Guide to Prioritizing in his book *Thinkertoys*. The technique, in simple terms, involves comparing each of the many alternatives that present themselves. The user will compare each pair of alternatives and decide which of the two is more attractive. This process repeats with each pair of choices. In the end the sum of times each option was picked will indicate the person's priorities. A renewable energy activist might decide to compare wind turbines, solar panels, biomass conversion, tide power, and geothermal power. He would compare each of the options against all of the others to see which of the pair is preferable. The most often selected technology would be the winner.

In this rather simple example, you can see solar photovoltaic power looks like the best focal point. Tide power, fuel cells, and OTEC (Ocean Thermal Energy Conversion) weren't chosen over anything else. Wind power was only chosen over fuel cells. This method of weighing your options will not make a decision for you, but it will indicate what you would really prefer to do. In many situations there would be more than four options to consider. This matrix method helps to reveal your preferences but cannot help you decide how to evaluate each pair of options.

Before you use this prioritizing tool you need to know why the options are desirable, so you can reasonably judge which option in each pair has more to offer. In the example above, ocean thermal energy conversion looks pretty good in comparison to most of the other choices. However, the selection process above did not take account of technological maturity. Some technologies are, at any given time, more suited for widespread use than other technologies. Ocean thermal energy conversion is not ready for wide use in late 2007, and may not be ready years. Solar, wind, and tide power generation are all relatively mature technologies, with solar and wind backed by huge networks of advocates, users, vendors, installers, and researchers.

The maturity of a technology should be an evaluation criterion where a technological solution is involved. That may seem obvious but sometimes our thinking can be led astray by ideas that seem really "cool" in some way. Consider hydrogen power for cars and utilities. It might seem clever and progressive to promote hydrogen power, but consider the relative immaturity of the technology. Consider public concerns over safety and the lack of any supporting infrastructure. What if something goes wrong with my hydrogen-powered car? What if nobody wants to buy my gasoline-to-hydrogen conversion kits?

Pros-Cons-Fixes

Sometimes you need to strengthen an existing idea, if that is possible. This is seemingly an easier situation than having to compare several pairs of alternatives as was done with the matrix method. A tool presented by Morgan D. James in *The Thinker's Toolkit* helps users improve on an idea.

Begin using Pros-Cons-Fixes by listing the positive points of an idea. Then list downsides or potential problems with each of the good things listed. The last step is to come up with fixes for as many of the cons as possible. This process should strengthen the idea unless this analysis reveals that the idea is unworkable.

Suppose we propose that the city government must begin purchasing only alternative fuel (alcohol, natural gas, electric, or bio-diesel) vehicles. Is that a good idea? How could the idea be strengthened? Take a few minutes to think about that idea. What are the pros? What might be wrong? How can those things be fixed. Then check the table on the following page:

Here is one possible breakdown of the pros, cons, and fixes:

Pros	Cons	Fixes
Reduces fossil fuel imports	Higher purchase price	Search for a grant, matching fund, or interest-free loan
Cleans the city's air	Higher fuel costs	Comparison shop for alternative fuels
Creates a market for alternative fuels	Higher maintenance costs	Search for matching funds

Other Peoples' Views

How will other people react to the new idea? What objections or concerns will they have? These are two questions that another of Edward De Bono's tools can help answer. Doing an OPV, in De Bono's terminology, means analyzing a situation or idea to determine how other affected people view things. Doing an OPV involves X steps

"Doing an OPV" is a process of considering how other people will react to an idea. While the necessity of doing that may seem obvious, it should also be obvious that people sometimes forget to consider how an idea will be received.   Several questions deserve to be answered. What are peoples' attitudes toward _____ (e.g., vegetarianism, sex education)? What concerns will people have about the impact of the idea? What factors will be of particular interest to your audience? Common factors of this sort include safety, privacy, independence, convenience, personal liberty, and general conservatism. Many people are biased against change, just because it is change.

Consequence and Sequel

What are the likely consequences if this idea is implemented? Are the consequences going to be negative or positive? These are two questions to answer using another of De Bono's thinking tools. To "do a C&S" on an idea means to consider the likely consequences at four points in time – the immediate future, the short term, the medium term, and the long term. De Bono suggests using one year for the immediate future, one to five years for the short term, five years and 20 years for the medium term, and over 20 years for the long term. Those time frames are only suggestions and can be modified to better suit a particular circumstance.

"Murder" Boards:

People shouldn't always check their own ideas. People tend to see the good points of their thinking and gloss over the weaknesses. We treat others' ideas in the same manner when we agree with the person's politics or religious views. This weakness is especially worrisome where decisions concerning public health and welfare are concerned. And most social and environmental issues do come down to concerns over public health or welfare. The sad state of mental health care for the poor and indigent is an obvious public welfare issue. Habitat destruction often produces a threat to human health and safety. When Hurricane Katrina struck New Orleans in August of 2005 the damage appears to have been magnified by the destruction of wetlands along the coastline.

Michael Michalko described the murder board in *Thinkertoys*. A murder board's function is to kill bad ideas. Apparently the forerunner of today's CIA introduced the murder board procedure in World War II. In any case, the process a murder board uses is perfectly well suited to evaluating ideas for social change, new policies, new social programs and similar "social betterment" tasks.

Begin the process by describing, in writing your idea. Define the issue you want to address, the source of the idea, the reasons why you are addressing the issue in question, and what sort of feedback you want. Do you want to ferret out the idea's weaknesses, decide how best to sell the idea, or something else? Describe the idea to someone you trust and get his or her reaction. Incorporate anything helpful into your written description, then show the idea to other people.

Simply put, a murder board is a group that subjects ideas to tough questions aimed at weeding out terrible ideas, strengthening marginal ideas, and providing detailed feedback on all ideas. In reality you would probably want to approach people one at a time and ask them for their feedback. You could, but don't have to, provide them with a list of specific questions to answer. Michalko provides a long list of suggested questions in *Thinkertoys*. The following list of (modified) questions will help you apply the murder board procedure to social betterment ideas:

- Does the idea really meet a need?
- Is the need felt by the audience now?
- Does it make sense to create a need for the idea?
- Does the idea offer any real and significant benefit?
- Who will resist this idea?
- Is the idea worth implementing, in terms of both time and money?
- How will the idea's implementation be funded?
- Will the benefits really outweigh the costs?
- What are the risks and are they acceptable?
- How will the idea be marketed?
- What objections will people raise to the idea?
- How can we respond to concerns or objections to the idea?
- Is timing a factor in marketing the idea?
- What is the competition for this idea?
- Is the idea sound?
- What are the limitations of this idea?
- Do you have the resources to implement this idea?
- Do you have the skills and knowledge to implement the idea?
- Why would the idea work in practice?

After collecting everyone's feedback you will evaluate the idea and decide whether or not to act on it. Michalko recommends assigning point values to each of eight factors that relate to the worthiness of your idea. The sum of the points gives a good quantitative indication of the idea's potential. The basic idea is easy to grasp. Marketability, personal competence, resources, personal interest, competitive advantage, distinctiveness, timing, and need all shape the idea's "implementability." Thinking explicitly about each factor will reveal where the idea needs to be improved, or if the idea needs to be scrapped.

Thought Experiments

A thought experiment is, in the simplest form, a way to ask a question and imagine the answer. Thought experiments can help people test ideas by revealing how the consequences of implementing the idea could play out. Einstein's famous speculation about riding a beam of light is probably the most famous thought experiment in the world. Philosophers and physicists sometimes use thought experiments to explore specific topics or research problems. People who want to change society in some way or improve society in some way can use thought experiments to explore the consequences of their ideas.

All thought experiments should begin with a specific question to answer. What would happen if...? Be specific about what happens in your experiment. "What if all of our homes made their own electricity?" is not as good as "What would happen if city building codes were changed to require new buildings and refurbished buildings to have solar cells capable of supplying at least 25% of the building's electricity needs. Any building not meeting that standard would have a pollution tax added to the annual property tax assessment. The pollution tax would be equal to the property tax."

The experiment should consider both immediate consequences and longer-term consequences. Maybe that new building regulation would have no effect because builders aren't responsible for the property tax and owners may prefer to pay the higher tax. Fitting enough solar cells and ancillary equipment would cost more. Suppose that doesn't happen, but the higher building cost leads to higher lease rates and a move out of the city to slightly cheaper suburbs.

Consider peoples' reactions, especially the behaviors that might change, new behaviors that might emerge, and old behaviors that might be dropped. Some informal reflection may have revealed negative reactions already. Conducting a thought experiment is a structured process for digging deeper into unintended consequences involving politics, economics, psychology, and culture. What might happen to relationships, in families for example, to the economy, or to social institutions like the school system, government, and religious institutions?

Maybe the proposed change will produce quantitative changes that can be characterized now. For example, the change might cause something to get bigger, smaller, more expensive, or more common. What broad sorts of changes might happen if the policy or program in question is implemented? Will the likely reactions tend to support or undermine things? Now is the time to identify these problems and modify your idea. Maybe a whole new idea is called for.

11 – Making the Best Decision

Everyone has to make decisions and most of us do a reasonably good job. Nevertheless, there will be occasions in the public sector where formal and systematic thinking about a decision is called for. In some cases a simple process is adequate. Write down the information that needs to be considered in the decision. Talk to one or two other knowledgeable people about the decision and what options you are considering. That information might be enough to indicate what decision is best, or at least reasonable.

Familiarity with a couple of decision making tools will make it easier to make good decisions. Decision analysis tools come in handy in three situations. One step in decision making is to decide what criteria define a good decision. These criteria might be revealed by a simple analysis of the situation, or in some cases a more sophisticated technique. AGO, FIP, Cost-Benefit Analysis, Fit, the Five Factors Method, Social Impact Assessment, C&S, MOST, and H2M can help you define decision criteria. Prioritizing, weighted ranking, and simple comparison can make it easier to choose between attractive alternatives.

AGO

A good decision requires knowledge of the goals and objectives the decision is expected to serve. This much is obvious. Sometimes some formal thinking on the goals and objectives involved is a worthwhile effort. The lateral thinking tool called AGO, for Aims-Goals-Objectives, is one tool for determining the appropriate goals and objectives for a social betterment effort. The essence of the technique is to spend a few minutes thinking about the aims, goals, and objectives of an project. A good decision will support one of those aims, goals, or objectives. Edward De Bono, the inventor of the technique notes that the distinction between aims, goals, and objectives is not important.

For practice, try to use AGO on this project: Establishing a YouTube video channel to promote your nonprofit.

Ban, Regulate, or Ignore

Sometimes the best approach to a social problem is to push for the source of the problem to be either banned or regulated. Sometimes the thing itself is best ignored. Whether it is more rational to try to ban something, or get it regulated, of just ignore it may not be obvious. You may have to acknowledge that the source of the problem is impossible to ban and impractical to regulate more, or at all.

Ban-Regulate-Ignore (BRI) is a tool for framing decisions like that. to determine the most efficient use of the organization's resources. The option that makes sense will depend on a impact and public concern. Impact depends on the social costs of a behavior.

Gun ownership is an example of something that can't realistically be banned in the United States. Advocating for new gun control rules may be more reasonable, but promises to be time-consuming and with no promise of success. Ignoring the fact the gun ownership is a "problem" in some sense may be the smart thing to do. In this way, nonprofits don't have to waste time and money on a "long shot" effort at banning all guns, banning handguns, or restricting how many guns a person can own.

Using this BRI trick can be as simple as reflecting on each option and scanning your own knowledge and experience. Can we really get disposable plastic bags banned? If so, will the effort be worth it relative to other efforts we could make at keeping plastic trash out of the river. If the stakes are high, a rigorous process of looking at the three options could be helpful.

All behaviors that might need to be regulated or banned have three characteristics in common: They all happen with some *frequency,* with some *impact* each time the behavior happens, and with various levels of *public concern* being raised. Frequency, impact, and public concern help determine whether banning, regulating or ignoring is the best approach.

If the frequency and the impact of each instance of a behavior is great and public concern is high, then pushing for a ban might make sense. If public concern is negligible, the behavior is rare, and the impact is minimal spending time and money to ban the behavior in question is not wise. Decision makers might wish to make a moral statement by trying to ban an activity, but this is rationally not the best use of resources. If the "problem" behavior doesn't trouble people in general, then trying the behavior will simply drain resources away from solving problems. What problems does the behavior cause? Identify one of those problems and try to address that.

What about things that are potentially dangerous? Guns, alcohol, and tobacco are easy examples of things that are inherently dangerous. Yet, none of those things can really hurt anyone. The behaviors associated with guns, alcohol, and tobacco can cause problems. It is not obvious that trying to ban tobacco products or tighten regulations on gun ownership are good uses of a nonprofit's resources.

BRI only works if the user knows something about the frequency, impact, and level of public concern related to the behavior or object.   There is no substitute for research, mainly research into existing statistics and survey results on the frequency and impact of a behavior or the risks associated with a thing like smokeless tobacco.

Public concern can be evaluated by the same kind of secondary research that will help you understand the impact of a problem. Think tanks, academic researchers, management consulting firms, advocacy groups, news organizations, and government agencies publish research on concern with certain social issues. Most of you have read about surveys reporting something like "The Top 5 Issues Facing the Nation."

What do we do about a product or service that seems to be harmful, or is actually harmful? How do we know if we should try to ban the thing in question, regulate it, or ignore it? We could ask five questions about the product, service, or behavior:

1.   How much of an impact does it have each time?
2.   How common is the thing we are concerned about?
3.   How common are the negative consequences?
4.   How concerned are people really?
5.   Is it something people are voluntarily exposed to?

These questions about how we should respond to one aspect of the issue provide one more tool is simply another thinking tool we can put in our intellectual toolbox. Even if there is no change of mind, people should come to better understand their reasoning behind a decision to push for regulation, for a ban, or to do nothing.

C&S

Consequence and Sequel (C&S) is useful for planning as well as for decision making. All decisions have consequences. The bigger the decision, the greater is the need to take a close look at the likely consequences. What are the likely consequences of implementing a particular decision? Consider the impact 1-year out, 5 years out, 10 years out and 20 years out. The time periods are generic and might need to be adjusted for some decisions. Consequence and Sequel helps reveal the likely effects of implementing a decision so the exercise can show whether the costs of implementing an idea are too great.

So, what do you need to think about when doing a C&S? Look for evidence of trends in popular culture, politics, the economy, technology, the environment, and demographics. Look for expert analysis of trends in those areas, after deciding which are most important to your cause. Research and conversations with experts will likely reveal things that were not clear from a casual consideration of the decision.

Cost-Benefit Analysis

Cost-benefit analysis is a complicated task with whole courses and books being created to describe the process. Instead, here is an argument for using it to make social betterment decisions: It should be obvious that all efforts by groups, individuals, and organizations impose costs. There is an investment of money of course, and this is the first sort of cost that comes to mind. Any activity also takes time, so the time needed (or predicted to be needed) is another cost. Opportunity costs, the membership fees, non-dues revenue, and social impacts, ought to be considered as well.

The plans in question are meant to have some benefit. What are the proposed benefits? A benefit should be quantified whenever possible: 160 families will be lifted out of poverty in the next 12 months.

Sometimes a qualitative assessment is all that's possible. Benefits that can't be readily expressed in numbers are sometimes more important than the hard numbers. Will a development project help preserve the historic character of a village? "Historic character" can't be assigned a number, but preserving the village's nature may be the most important thing.

Decisions should not be made by the results of a cost-benefit analysis. The analysis should and will yield clearer thinking about how the organization's resources can be deployed to best advantage. After all, the social sector has money and people to devote to their work, but the organization's resources are limited.

Devil's Advocacy

This is a simple tool for problem analysis, one that most readers will be familiar with. The less formal process of looking for reasons that X may not be true or may not be a good idea is the version most familiar to us. Our new friend Morgan D. Jones offers a rather more systematic approach to playing the devil's advocate:

1. List evidence that supports the proposal.
2. List available evidence that contradicts the proposal.
3. List evidence that is not available, but would support the proposal.

The point of this little exercise is to force the user to go beyond a built-in bias to focus on confirming the value of our own ideas by overlooking contradictory evidence and arguments. Arguments can be used in place of or in addition to factual evidence. What arguments support the proposal in question? What arguments refute the proposal?

FIP

Decision analysis will be easier if it starts with a clear picture of the organization's priorities. So, what are the organization's priorities, and how are they ordered? Knowing the organization's real priorities, in rough order of their importance, makes many decisions easier.

Priorities may be internal to the organization or external. Internal priorities include things like fundraising efforts and hiring. External priorities correspond to goals and objectives. A nonprofit with several programs aimed at addressing the effects of extreme poverty may have several issues to deal with. Issues like lack of access to credit, chronic disease, illiteracy, and other factors keep people in poverty. Not all of those factors can be given the same level of attention. What is the organization's First Important Priorities in such a situation?

"Fit"- ness

All decisions have to implemented in some type of social environment. Five general considerations need to factor into a decision:

1. How well does the idea fit with prevailing cultural norms? If there is a serious mismatch the idea should probably be dropped.
2. How well does the idea fit with the political climate? In a religious society, any idea that conflicts with religious beliefs. If the

economy is terrible, the expensive but powerful idea should get some demerits.

3. How will you get people or their representatives to support an expensive idea with uncertain impacts?

4. How easy is it to implement the idea using widely available technology? Any idea that depends heavily on new or expensive technology may be too difficult to implement.

5. Are there any ecological costs? This is an important element of a successful idea since environmental concerns factor in to so many decisions by individuals, governments, and businesses.

The MOST Effective Approach

Implementing any decision implies an investment of time, money, and reputation. Reputation can be enhanced or reduced by the outcome of a decision. We mostly recognize this fact in our personal lives, maybe less so in organizations. Decision-makers in organizations do need to pay attention to the reputation of their organization and also on how decisions will reflect on the organization.

Consider organizing your thoughts on the costs of a decision by using the acronym MOST (Money-Opportunity-Status-Time). *Money* naturally represents the money required to implement a decision. Money could be cash or in-kind contributions. *Opportunity* costs are what's lost by implementing a certain decision. *Status* refers to the likely impact on the organization or group's reputation. *Time* is the staff time or volunteer time that would be required.

Reputation or status can be enhanced or damaged in two ways. A decision will be seen as consistent with or inconsistent with the real or perceived goals of an organization The actual effects of a decision are also going to be judged, if not by the public then by certain important constituents. Students, parents of students, potential donors, and staff at other nonprofits, leaders in other communities – to name a few of those other constituents – are watching. A smart decision would be one that takes account of the impact of that decision on the organization's reputation.

All decisions that are acted upon have to be acted upon to the exclusion of something else. What else could have been done with the time and money invested? What value relative to that gain are you getting by doing what you actually decided to do? This is what is meant by *opportunity costs*, a sometimes-overlooked concept from economics. If the decision is relatively minor relative to the organization's resources then considering the opportunity costs in a systematic way isn't really necessary. The goal of thinking about opportunity costs is to decide whether option X will give the most benefit for the time and money invested.

Opportunity costs could be compared for just about anything, though there is no reason to waste time on costs that lie outside of your are of interest. Would the community be more improved if there were a new community center and a playground, or if there were recycling bins in every neighborhood? A community group is almost always going to be organized around one goal, such as improving local quality of life.

Social Impact

Considering the social impact of a decision is just another way of forecasting likely consequences of the decision. What is likely to happen? What could go wrong? How likely is each of the risks and how severe would each event be? These questions could be answered using a relatively simple thought experiment, a group brainstorming session, a scan of one's own experience, or consultation with experts. An experience scan could be done as a group exercise, as a different sort of brainstorming session.

The social impacts of a decision could be felt inside an organization as well as in the wider community. Which to focus depends on where the decision will be implemented. An internal decision on program priorities is one that could affect both the social environment and the organization.

A thought experiment is really an informal way of reflecting on what might logically happen in a given situation. The outcome of a decision could be derived by reflected on experience, knowledge of the social sciences, and reflections on human nature. Project the likely economic, political, cultural, and psychological changes that might happen as result of implementing the decision.

Don't work alone when evaluating the social impact of a big decision. Make it a group brainstorming session or a group problem-solving session. The proper techniques are similar in either case. In this case the issue is the likely social impact of implementing a decision. This can be done for decisions being contemplated by the group, by an opposition group, or by the government. The latter two uses should not be hard to understand. An unfavorable analysis of the other side's idea would provide ammunition for an opposition campaign. Everyone could get two or three minutes to generate as many thoughts as possible. Try using this framework to organize each member's thinking about likely social impacts:

1. *Culture* – norms, values, attitudes, social relations, lifestyle.

2. *Ecology* – air, water, soil, forests, et cetera.

3. *Demography* – people and their characteristics

4. *Technology* – usage rates, trends, risks, issues.

5. *Legal* – time and cost impact of new laws, and regulations.

6. *Economic* – taxes, jobs, employment rates, and income.

7. *Politics* – power, changing political climate, costs.

Not all elements will apply in all cases, but it makes sense to give a little attention to each.

The experience scan is another of De Bono's thinking tools. The general idea is simple enough - spend some time thinking about things that have happened or things the person has learned, whether through direct experience or education. Things that have happened to other organizations, communities, or groups are also sources of experience. The experience scan should yield more insight into the likely consequences of a decision. Talk to experts about the decision. The more complex the situation, and the greater the investment for your organization the more sense it makes to talk to a few experts. These could be academics, experienced activists, nonprofit managers used to dealing with an issue, or government officials. Freelance writers and journalists with a detailed knowledge of the subject matter are a great source of information.

Local colleges and universities are a good place to look for a little free or cheap advice. An online service like authorsandexperts.com can also point you to an expert in the relevant subject. Try a few sources of expert advice and see how things work out. You might be surprised at what a short search can turn up by way of expertise and statistical data that supports your analysis.

Use this simplified form of social impact assessment to predict whether or not the idea will have acceptable social costs. If your own idea comes out looking good, then it is probably worth implementing. The outcomes of this analysis could be used against another group, or to choose which of a few likely ideas should be implemented. Or, the analysis could be applied to one idea so you know whether the idea is really a good one.

Five Factors

A good decision is one that will produce the desired results. A decision is more likely to be a good one when certain factors are considered. Five factors seem especially relevant to the nonprofit world: public opinion, frequency of behaviors, the impact of the behavior, knowledge (of how to influence the behavior), ability of the organization   to influence events. The factors can be used as a type of sanity check - "Is this really a big problem or do we just think so? - as well as a tool to guide serious analysis of how best to tackle a social problem.

- *Public Opinion* – How much does the public care about the behavior in question? How much they "should" care is irrelevant, because this attitude suggests a public education or advocacy campaign is called for, not a decision to directly attack some behavior.
- *Frequency* – How often does the behavior in question happen? This could be defined in many ways really. It makes sense to talk about the number of smokers or the rate at which teenagers become new smokers. Thinking in terms of the number of times people in the United States light up does not make as

much sense.

- *Magnitude* - How serious is it each time the behavior in question occurs?
- *Knowledge* – Is there sufficient knowledge available to effectively influence the behavior in question?
- *Ability* – This is not a philosophical question. Does the organization or group in question have the resources necessary to effectively attack the behavior in question.

An effort to address teen drug abuse, will illustrate how the five factors can be used in real decisions. Let's say that four drugs cause most of our concern. The challenge here is to decide which drug or drugs, need to be focused on. The five factors, the four drugs, and ratings on each factor might be summarized as follows.

A similar table could be used in any location, for any sort of problem. Just replace the drugs with, for example, specific environmental issues or mental health problems. Do the needed research on frequency, impact and so forth. Complete the table and evaluate the options. While your choice of focus may not change, you are now better prepared to defend your decision and better able to judge that the chosen area of focus is reasonable.

Factor	Meth	Alcohol	Crack	Tobacco
Frequency	1	3	2	4
Magnitude	4	1	3	2
Concern	2	3	4	1
Knowledge	1	3	2	4
Ability	2	4	1	3

The *frequency* is ranked from 4 (most common) to 1 (least common) and is based on published estimates of the rate at which a behavior occurs. In other sorts of decisions another measure of frequency might be more appropriate. You could use percentages or rates per 1,000 or 100,000 people to give two examples.

Magnitude is measured by the health consequences and is ranked from 1 to 4. Ranking these items takes significant knowledge, or at least the desire to do significant research. This judgement is based on the opinions of experts who have investigated impacts of each substance. In this case, as in most uses of this tool, magnitude measures the impact on the individual. Tobacco use is considered more harmful than alcohol and less harmful than crack cocaine or meth.

Public *concern* is based on ranking the drugs according to the percentage of people who consider the problem "Serious" or "Very Serious" with a 4 representing the highest level of concern. You could use published survey data here, or make educated guesses. The problem with guessing isn't the fact that you are guessing; it is the fact that the "guesses" might be your opinion of how much people should care about each drug. You need to discuss possible rankings with other people and get some agreement on how much people care about each of the drugs.

Knowledge relates to the existence of programs to address that particular issue and their success rate if any such information exists. Knowledge is also ranked from 1 to 4. Ties are possible. Do not rely on anecdotal evidence like testimonials and case studies here. Use expert evaluations and scholarly research to identify successful drug treatment programs before deciding what to implement.

Ability refers to a practical ability to implement a program or policy that will affect the behavior in question. In this case, "ability" means the ability to implement a program that will reduce the frequency of use of the targeted substance. The program could be one of direct impact, like distributing public education materials to parents, or it could be something with an indirect impact like lobbying for a stronger anti-drug education effort in schools. Again, the target would be one selected substance. Ability is also ranked 1 to 4 and ties are possible.

The rankings appear to support two conclusions. Assume that all of the factors are ranked accurately and on the same scale. If you add the ranks, what drug should be the one we focus on, i.e. the one with the highest score? Alcohol is the "winner" in this comparison. However, tobacco comes in at #2 with a score of 12. The other two drugs both score an "11" so they really aren't far behind. In this case, the conclusion we draw is that alcohol use deserves exclusive attention only a little more than tobacco, which deserves exclusive attention only a little more than crack and crystal meth. Remember: These are rankings and not real scores, so a "score" of 12 isn't twice as much as a six.

Sometimes it make sense to eliminate public concern from the evaluation. It could make sense to do so if the problem is hard to understand since people tend to tune out complex problematic issues. Anyway, public concern over an issue often has no relationship at all to the issue's quantifiable significance. Public concern *should* be a factor if you want people to either vote on something or change a particular behavior. If people don't think X is a problem why will they go to the trouble to change my behavior to help combat X?

Be careful that this system does not become a way to justify the outcome you want. Say you are convinced that crystal meth is the biggest drug problem facing teens and something must be done. Your assessment of magnitude, knowledge, and ability, and concern will lead meth to look like the best target. That sort of problem can be mitigated in three ways:

1. Work with one or more people on this exercise.
2. Have someone play devil's advocate.
3. Write down your ideas.

H2M Technique

Comparing the possibilities on three dimensions can do comparing alternative objectives for an organization or program or policy, or targets for an effort. Many social issues have effects on health – mental and physical – and budgets. This technique could best be used in the early stages of trying to deal with a social issue, such as when deciding on a n approach that an organization can take to solving a problem. Different options for addressing a challenge will have different outcomes relative to the mental health, physical health, and the financial impacts of a social issue. Not all elements of every social issue will have the same impacts.

Prioritizing

Not every good idea can be used at once, of course. Deciding what to do first, and why, can be a tough decision. Prioritizing tasks is something people often do when planning their workday or workweek. A similar process can help you choose between several good ideas or several objectives. Not all objectives can be pursued at once, except maybe in rare instances. It is much more realistic to choose one objective and start working toward that. Depending on the scale of operations and the organization's resources it could obviously be possible to pursue two or three objectives at once.

This is a good method to use in choosing between many options when there is only time or money for one thing. As the name implies, you would make comparisons between each possible pair of options. The number of times a certain option gets chosen over the alternate option, the higher the priority of acting on that option. This method only suggests which option should be pursued first, or in exclusion to all others. You still need to do a sanity check to make sure there is nothing seriously wrong with your choice.

To illustrate a social change application of this method let's return to the renewable energy example from Chapter 7. Suppose that we only have the resources needed to promote one technology out of the several realistic possibilities that now exist. How do we decide what to do? Suppose our renewable energy options are solar photovoltaic, biodiesel, small-scale wind turbines, ethanol from corn, and methane from agricultural waste.

As always, we still need to decide on some criteria, otherwise there is no good reason to pick one thing over another. We are going on gut reactions, personal bias, and maybe aesthetic or ideological preference. Ideology and aesthetics need to be supplemented by other considerations too: Technical considerations, fit with the local culture, appropriateness for the local infrastructure and natural environment, political feasibility, economic viability, and legal compliance. Paired comparisons can lead you to an option that most deserves this in-depth study of the acceptability.

Evaluating Alternative Fuel Options

Options	ethanol	methane	solar	wind	biodiesel
ethanol					
methane				X	X
solar	X	X		X	X
wind					
biodiesel				X	

You could set up a table like the one below and mark an X when we would choose the option on the left over any option shown in the row headings. Just count the 'X's' to identify the best focal point.

We can choose an option in several other ways. An analysis of the technologies – cost, maturity, current infrastructure – could yield a clear winner without any other form of decision analysis being needed. Maybe we are both intimately familiar with solar photovoltaic power applications but less familiar with all of the others. That familiarity strongly suggests the most reasonable focus.

Who really wants to evaluate all seven of those renewable energy options for their usefulness in a certain region, city, or town? It makes better sense to pare down the candidate technologies to one that is most appealing for whatever reason. A more-rigorous study of that technology can then proceed. Maybe one or two serious flaws in this choice appear. Maybe those flaws can be overcome by a little creative thinking, or perhaps another renewable energy option needs to be selected.

The point of advocacy is to create some change in society, or at least in the small part of it most relevant to the activists in question. Whether you want to achieve some concrete change or simply change peoples' minds about an issue, several decision analysis tools can help to get the best results for a given effort. (And who says that changing minds is simple!). Deciding on a focus for an effort is obviously something that someone does when getting involved in social change. What cause should the group tackle? What change or changes do we support? What is the first action step? The Five Factors can help you define a sensible focus for your efforts on one of several possibilities. The results could also be used to "sell" action by others by showing what problem or aspect of a big problem is most amenable to improvement. Before promoting a specific idea it might be wise to do a C&S on the idea. Are those the consequences you hoped for? What problem does the exercise reveal and how you solve each problem *before* implementing the idea?

Addressing those potential problems could be relatively simple, or effectively impossible. Doing a thought experiment would serve the same purpose. Formal problem analysis and some brainstorming may need to be applied. BRI can help you refine your thinking on whether a targeted behavior, product, service, or business practice should be banned, regulated, or ignored. BRI could be used informally or as a structure for thorough analysis of secondary research data. Likewise, H2M organizes an assessment of how significant each element of a problem really is.

Whether in a school or as a public education effort, we obviously want to make good decisions about how our resources are used. Public education (tied to specific advocacy goal or not): Five Factors helps determine what people need education about. Concern about one aspect of a problem, such as teen substance abuse, may lag far behind what the actual impacts suggest public concern should be. A cost-benefit analysis, even an informal one, will help you make a better decision about how to use the organization's resources. Doing an AGO will help to clarify the real point of an education initiative. That exercise will lead to better decisions about advertising, budgeting, and curriculum design.

Policies are mostly something to "sell" to politicians, executives, and voters. Some readers will be in a position to contribute to, or even write, policies for organizations. In either case, the same decision analysis advice applies. Use Ban-Regulate-Ignore to determine the best approach to a "problem" behavior. Maybe something will turn out to be of minor importance when analyzed systematically and objectively. It makes sense to find this out beforehand so resources can be deployed more effectively. Cost-Benefit analysis will help to reveal the facts about a policy's impact relative to the cost. H2M can reveal the real costs in time, mental health, and physical health of a social problem. Maybe the problem in question isn't even worth attacking through formal policies. Maybe an opportunity will yield too few benefits for the time and money to be invested. Use H2M in conjunction with CBA to clarify the best uses for the organization's time and money.

Using Five Factors can help policy folks decide how to deploy society's resources, or the organization's resources. After all, that is what a real policy does; it directs people in spending time and money on some things rather than on others. What behaviors should be addressed to have maximum impact? This is a good question to ask whether the point is to solve a problem or exploit some opportunity.

On a broader scale the use of society's resources to implement and to enforce a policy needs to be managed responsibly and effectively. Honest opinions on what that means can vary, but the point is to have some objective foundation on which to base a judgement. This sort of thing lays the foundation for informed criticism of opposing ideas and for critical analysis of one's own policy ideas. Using relatively objective empirical data to decide on policy directions also helps avoid unproductive debates over who has the best idea or the most concern for the public.

Politicians usually care more about reelection and their party's agenda than they care about the public interest. FMCKA can be used on politicians in two ways. Use your analysis to show how wrong the politician's ideas really are, or how good they are if you support that politician. Publicize the benefits of your organization's idea.

Applying decision analysis tools to other peoples' ideas can have two benefits. It can reveal that the idea is really sound, in some sense of that term. The logical response to this finding is to go on and do something else. Or, unfavorable results can be publicized in an effort to defeat the other side, or to shame them into working on something new. If the outcomes of your decision analysis exercises are really negative, the shaming approach may just be worthwhile.

Program decisions happen before the program even gets started and as things proceed effectively, or not so effectively. Deciding how to proceed or whether to implement a proposed change are different tasks.

When the program exists, the point of decision analysis is to make a wise decision regarding operations, in some sense of that term. Does the program continue, get expanded, or get cut back in scale or time? You may be involved in making the final decision, or in recommending a course of action, or in "selling" a certain course of action. Advocacy groups, unions, and community groups are especially likely to face that sort of decision-making situation.

Aside from major questions about the existence of a program, there are usually minor decisions to make about program operations. Using CBA can help determine if a program is likely to give results consistent with the resources invested. Using FMCKA can help focus program efforts, or refocus them if the results haven't been as hoped for. A program, policy, or project idea should always, repeat *always*, pass a sanity test. Doing an AGO can reveal your real hopes for the proposed program. The physical health, mental health, and financial impacts of things that the program could perhaps should) try to address can also be calculated as decision time approaches.

11 – Collaborating for Change

People should form groups to solve problems and take advantage of opportunities. Of course there are already group brainstorming sessions and strategic planning sessions. Many groups and organizations use online collaboration tools, including blogs and wikis to foster collaboration and coordination. Many people know how to set up some sorts of effective collaborations and coordination. Ongoing collaborative efforts in real groups and in virtual groups are even better than one-shot group exercises. This chapter is about a range of tools designed specifically to foster collaboration on idea generation or on problem solving. Let's start with a concept introduced by Edward de Bono decades ago.

Action Groups

An action group is like a mastermind group, in the sense that people are getting together to work on some issue. The ideal size for an action group is three to six people. In an action group the point is to use some tool or tactic or technique to promote a shared cause. The members might work with other group members or only with a distinct group or organization. The point is to build a group that focuses on doing something specific with a particular tool or technique as a central part of the effort. Each member of the group will take on specific tasks between meetings.

An action group could be centered on using lateral thinking, Einstein thinking or problem analysis applied to a particular goal.

Activists can use action groups to work on a particular agenda in the areas of public education or advocacy or political campaigns. In fact this is another legitimate realm for activism – getting voters to support a certain candidate is hardly a new activism strategy. Any issue area is certainly amenable to formation of an action group. An action group is about cooperating on means, whereas a mastermind group is built around related goals or identical goals. Educators interested in reform or in improved teaching techniques or in new programs or policies could form action groups. Nonprofit managers could form action groups to practice problem-solving techniques that could assist with fundraising, program success, and volunteer recruitment.

Cloud 9 File

The Cloud 9 file is another "idea collecting" procedure first suggested by Edward De Bono in *Serious Creativity*. A physical file would be circulated among executives, senior managers, or administrators depending on the organization. In a geographically dispersed organization, or simply a very large one, a wiki could be used instead of a physical file. Here is what Edward De Bono suggests that a "Cloud 9" file should include:

- *Novel Ideas* – these ideas are already in use somewhere, perhaps in another type of organization but could be adapted to your organization
- *Original Ideas* – these ideas are truly new as far as the author knows
- *Constructive Comments* – including information for or suggestions for improvements related to an idea

- *New Creative Focuses* – Suggested things that need creativity applied; policies, programs, classes, marketing, fundraising, and other areas specific to different sorts of organizations.

This is different from idea management in that the same material keeps circulating, whereas idea management is focused on a project.

A message board on a nonprofit or education site could also become a Cloud 9 file of sorts. The main topics could be specific areas of focus where new ideas are needed. Each topic is one area, and each reply and reply to a reply becomes a section of the Cloud 9 file.

Concept R&D

Concept research and development is another Edward De Bono concept, also introduced in *Serious Creativity*. The process involves looking for concepts, general ways of doing things, which can be developed into practical ideas. The ideas can follow directly from a concept or a concept can be analyzed to yield a higher level concept. The higher level concept could lead to new lower level concepts and to new, specific ways of doing things.

Concept research and development could proceed from a concept map. The map should yield practical ideas that could be refined and implemented by the sponsoring organization. The most fertile ground for new concepts is probably going to be areas outside the usual "realm" inhabited by people working on social betterment. Look to areas like publishing, architecture, advertising, public relations, real estate, graphic design, or almost any other area of human activity. What could an international humanitarian relief agency discover by examining the concepts used by advertisers? It might be worthwhile to find out.

What becomes of ideas that come out of this process? The ideas should be treated in the usual way by evaluating them, refining them, and combining them. Implementation naturally follows. Implementation could proceed at full-scale or as a trial or a pilot project.

Creative Hit List

The creative hit list is another idea presented in *Serious Creativity*. A Creative Hit List is simply a list of problems, general opportunities, improvement opportunities, and projects. There could also be subject areas submitted for consideration just because the list owner is interested in getting some new ideas on the subject. This list offers more details on how the categories of Creative Hit List items could be used for social betterment:

Problems – subjects requiring some creative input, as opposed to investigation and analysis, that are concrete and specific to the organization. Problem areas could include success rates in programs, recruiting volunteers, retaining volunteers, compliance with new regulations, or coping with budget shortfalls.

General Opportunities – New technologies, processes, programs (such as the federal government's Energy Star ® program for energy efficiency), funding sources, seminars, conferences, training opportunities, and software could all be recorded here. Some types of organizations will have other specific opportunities that are relevant to them. These things could be used to some advantage by the organization, but only if the right people are aware of them.

Project – Fundraising efforts, new class or program development, new public education campaigns and other work with a defined beginning, end, and work product. These projects could have started as a result of something on the creative hit list, or could be projects planned for another reason.

Improvement Opportunity – Programs, internal policies, advocacy tactics, fundraising techniques, and recruiting tactics could be working well, and yet there is room for improvement.

There could be one list for the organization, one for each location, one for each member organization in a network, or whatever division scheme makes sense. Individuals could even maintain their own creative hit lists. The lists could be shared in a wiki if the group is geographically dispersed. The Innovation Center could supervise the list or lists.

Creative Task Sheet

This technique for soliciting creative ideas was developed by Edward Be Bono and described in *Serious Creativity*. The Creative Task Sheet is a list of assignments for individual staff members. The point of each including each item on the list is to get ideas from a specific individual. Each item is assigned to that individual with the assignment to develop new ideas for improving, implementing, selling, or designing whatever is on the organization's "radar" screen at that time. The person responsible for the project or other effort in question could distribute a Creative Task Sheet in question. Or, the need for ideas could be routed through the Innovation Center. The instructions could request new concepts, new designs, alternatives, suggestions, problem analysis, or even research or analysis. The Task Sheet could include suggestions on the techniques to use, following the guide in Chapter 16 on what to use in what circumstances.

Computer-savvy readers may have noticed that a creative task sheet could be distributed electronically. Why bother with routing a paper file around an office, or between offices in different locations! Those simple word processing files mentioned in the Brainstorming chapter could be shared by email. Users of most brainstorming software can share the output with people who don't have the software. Export the output into a word processing document.

Email communications can become hard to organize and track though. A collaborative Web site might be a better option. Software like Lotus Team WorkPlace can be used to easily organize ideas into categories.

Innovation Center

This idea is inspired by the creativity center proposed by Edward De Bono in *Serious Creativity*. An Innovation Center is really an office or informal group changed with collecting, organizing, and publicizing creative efforts. In an organization the creative center could engage in its own work through concept research, action groups, or the application of any creative thinking tools. An Innovation Center could take two basic forms, depending on the organization that establishes it. In a very large and well-funded organization a formal office with a staff and budget could be established. It doesn't even need to be called The Innovation Center, any name that suggests its purpose will do. In a network of smaller organizations an innovation center could be a small group of people, staff or volunteers, who share the work.

The Innovation Center could be purely for planning and research or could have an operational role. In this role, the center would organize efforts to implement innovations. Staff members should be process champions for ideas, or at least that role should be assigned to someone else in the organization. The Center could also coordinate training on creativity, problem analysis, and decision analysis. Of course, the Innovation Center would never become the organization's sole source of new ideas and innovations. Some of the other structures or processes described in this chapter should also be implemented. Informally innovation efforts and suggestions should remain part of the organization's efforts.

Opportunity Search

Organizations tend to focus on problems to solve, and sometimes on potential problems. This makes sense because problems are, for want of a better term, problematic. We have to do something or suffer the consequences. However, all organizations have opportunities to improve good programs, raise more money, start new programs, and achieve other things. The point is to search for these opportunities and take advantage of them. This might not happen as much as it could unless searching for opportunities and acting on them becomes a formalized part of the organization's operations.

Opportunity searches could be organized in two ways. Each division or program in an organization could be responsible for finding and exploiting relevant opportunities. Better yet: One specific person in management would be responsible for that group's efforts. The responsible people would have to report regularly on opportunities found, actions taken, and the results. In some cases the report would constitute a progress report on some small project that's still underway. In other cases an opportunity could be identified but nothing is done because of lack of time, money, or necessary expertise. Those situations also need to be reported, not to fix blame on anyone but to see if any changes need to be made in the organization's use of resources.

Social Networking Sites

Social networking sites are hugely popular and are almost certain to remain so. Why are they relevant to social betterment ideas? LinkedIn is the go-to site for business networking and information sharing in 2020. Join the site, and join some groups. If there isn't a group for your cause or challenge, create one. Pose creative thinking challenges for members or discuss problem-solving strategies. Brainstorm together via Zoom or Google Hangouts.

LinkedIn and other social networking sites might also be useful for crowdsourcing: create a group that's organized around a particular challenge and encourage people to submit ideas, information, or analysis. Contribute ideas, critique ideas, try to combine or improve ideas and invite other group members to do the same.

Project Books

A project book is simply a written record of a project. It

contains information on what resources were helpful, who helped, how they helped, what problems were encountered and how they were handled, and some identifying information about the project. This is how a project book would be used in business. In the social sector a project book would be used in the same way. Record what was done, how it worked, what problems were encountered, and how the problems were solved. You'll also need to list helpful resources whether they were people, books, or Web sites. The project book can be an actual note-book, or a Web page, or an electronic document. Sharing project books with other organizations is a good idea. The point of creating a project book is to record the knowledge acquired in the course of the project so this knowledge is readily available to others.

Crowdsourcing

No modern discussion of group brainstorming would be complete without a mention of how the Web can be used to reach out to problem solvers. Crowdsourcing is just what the name implies. A challenge can be put out on the Web for the benefit of anyone who wants to offer a suggestion. There are a few ways to engage in crowdsourcing. Perhaps the easiest method starts with a blog post. Use the blog post to describe the challenge and solicit ideas. Readers can use the comments section to offer ideas and discuss or evaluate. Someone at the organization can moderate the discussion as needed.

A Website called Freelancer.com offers the ability to create a contest, instead of a job listing. A contest could offer a small prize for the best new idea. At least one site designed just for crowdsourcing innovation, called Icon, does exist in late 2013.

It might be helpful to get the public or a segment of it involved in developing approaches to a particular challenge. Crowdsourcing is one tool an organization could use. This is Wikipedia's definition of crowdsourcing: "Crowdsourcing is a ... business model in which a company or institution takes a job traditionally performed by a designated agent (usually an employee) and outsources it to an undefined, generally large group of people in the form of an open call over the Internet..."

Any nonprofit with a Web presence and a good web designer could, in theory, make good use of crowdsourcing. Some organizations and causes are going to be better uses of crowdsourcing than others are. Why do you need online input into a local advocacy campaign? Why not rely on people and organizations you already know? Any effort that has a huge geographic reach or a hugely complex problem to address may benefit from crowdsourcing.

No specific software for crowdsourcing appears to exist, but some Web sites might prove useful. Cambrian House is a crowdsourcing community that people can join to submit ideas or work on existing ideas with others. Jwiki offers a reasonably simple tool that people can use to create wikis. Global Ideas Bank offers a potentially useful forum for trying out ideas. Members can post ideas and get ratings of their feasibility, as well as specific critical comments from other members.

A nonprofit or network of nonprofits could develop a crowdsourcing site. People could be encouraged to work for recognition, for a prize (following the lead of Global Ideas Bank) or for money. Crowdsourcing sites could focus on a general area of interest to the creators, such as promoting renewable energy or promoting tolerance of homosexuals. The site could also change focus as needs dictate or there could be several campaigns running at the same time. Creating a crowdsourcing site with the huge number of pages and the interactive pages (probably with accounts and secure logins) is an advanced project to be sure!

Crowdsourcing seems to be an Internet phenomenon but the Internet isn't strictly necessary. Whenever a large group of relatively diverse people gathers in the real world there is an opportunity to "recruit" peoples' help with an issue. The other essential elements in this form of crowdsourcing are a large (very large!) area for people to write on and a short, clear statement of the issue. People can be instructed on what to do and how to interact with other peoples' ideas. The most likely methods are to initial your creation so other people can refer to the idea easily: "I like JK's idea and think it would be even better if you also did _____." Paste up some huge sheets of paper around the edge of an exhibition area or a big meeting room that gets plenty of traffic through the week Leave the paper, dry erase boards, or whatever exposed to the public for a few weeks. Collect the writings and see what people came up with.

Why not set up a telephone system to serve as a crowdsourcing medium? Admittedly, a web site would probably be easier to create and accessible to enough people. In poor parts of the world a wall or a large bulletin board space could be used. In urban settings these things would be too vulnerable to vandalism. Still, in rural communities where literacy is not too low, a central public location might be realistically used to gather ideas in a big meeting.

Activists can work together on a global issue that calls for many local actions, such as confronting global climate change. A local issue that happens to be common to lots of different localities would offer an obvious chance for crowdsourcing to work.

In-person brainstorming sessions using a formal technique or an informal process of soliciting ideas would work for the same issues, or for something local – "How can we convince the voters to uphold a ban on handgun ownership in the city?" Activist groups may need new ideas for publicity stunts.

Activists could use the Web to solicit ideas from the general public *on certain sorts of issues*. Issues that affect, or at least interest, populations that have a very high level of Internet access are most amenable to activist crowdsourcing. More and more progressive types and professional activists are Net savvy these days. So, it may already be true that pretty much any issue can be addressed through crowdsourcing.

Two cautions are in order. *First*, the population who is most likely to be attracted to a certain effort may be a population of people who generally think alike on social issues or environmental issues or whatever. This can reduce the quality of the ideas, or the chance of coming up with a practical, breakthrough idea. *Second*, people with great ideas or information may not have access to the Internet, or they may not be comfortable with computers. Lack of access and lack of comfort are almost certain to pose problems outside of highly developed nations.

Idea Management

Think of a suggestion box. Now think of a suggestion box that's online, controlled and reviewed by people, and used for a specific campaign, or challenge. That's the basic idea behind idea management. Idea management is usually talked about in conjunction with the software used to manage the whole process of soliciting and reviewing ideas. The software is typically installed on servers and accessed through a Web browser. It is also possible to use software hosted on the vendor's server.

Companies like Brainbank®, Jennie®, and OVO® make idea management software. The features and interface design vary but certain features are pretty typical. First, the software is designed around campaigns. The client sets up a project intended to solicit ideas on a specific subject. The subject could be rather broad – "We need ideas for promoting our safer sex programs." or rather more specific – "We need ways to increase our fundraising by 25% this holiday season." Idea management software also tends to have two sections, one for administration and one for idea generation. Managers can review other peoples' ideas. The software generally has some work-flow functionality: Ideas are routed from a submission form to a repository to a reviewer or reviewers, and confirmation emails are sent to the idea submitter.

While idea management software can be powerful it is also expensive and complicated. In some cases the cost and complexity can be justified. A huge organization like Amnesty International or United Way should be able to get value from an investment in idea management software. A distributed network of small organizations and advocacy groups might be able to share the cost and get some advantages.

Advocacy

Activists need to come up with ideas, advertise their ideas, and get people to accept their ideas. A mastermind group could certainly help with all three goals. Concept research could help with the latter.

Advocacy for a certain policy or program may require coming up with something new and effective. This is another area where concept research could be useful, as could an innovation center. The innovation center could be formally organized as a unit of a larger organization or it could be an informal group/network. The center would be tasked with creating new policy ideas, new concepts to work with, new ways of putting the concepts into action, and new tactics for the organization. Activists need to stop sometimes and look for new opportunities to spread their message. This is a common enough practice but it should be a formal, regularly scheduled activity. Large organizations could use Cloud 9 files and creative hit lists to work on ways to get better results.

Fundraising

Development people and fundraising professionals should really consider mastermind groups. Organizations often have complementary or identical goals, perhaps focusing on different areas of a state or nation. Those organizations don't compete for donors, especially if they focus on different cities or regions. Non-competing organizations should benefit if their staff start mastermind groups focused on fundraising. The same advice naturally applies to pursuit of in-kind contributions and to generating non-dues revenue. Somewhere there are better ideas for small organizations than the standard bake sale, car wash, or raffle.

Policy and Program Development

Policy and program innovation represent two areas where concept research, opportunity searches, creative hit lists, and Cloud 9 files are badly needed. Looking for new policy tools requires problem definition, analysis, research, and creativity. Selling the policy and program ideas would take some legwork and creativity too. Perhaps groups with a common interest, such as sustainable development, need to jointly operate an innovation research center that looks at opportunities, researches new concepts, studies problems, and brainstorms.

Sustained efforts require collaboration across a few weeks to months and sometimes across considerable distances. Listservs, regular teleconferences, and message boards aren't quite the same as software designed to facilitate brainstorming by large groups, when the individual members have the time, and without the need to assemble people in one location. Idea management software can save time and money for schools. Crowdsourcing can create better ideas by opening challenges to input by students, parents, and anyone else who finds the challenge interesting. On a somewhat more modest scale, an organization could use group brainstorming people to connect people who might have trouble getting together to brainstorm in person. Some of the interested employees could easily get together and use a structured brainstorming technique.

Nonprofits and some schools try to raise money. Student groups try to raise money too. Crowdsourcing might help them all. "How do we raise money in new ways that will really get the attention of our target audience?" Fundraising letters, Internet appeals, and car washes are all fine, as far as they go. Maybe new ideas will bring better results. At worst, a wild but reasonable idea might get some free press coverage. Free press coverage might lead to better fundraising results.

Fundraisers also need strategies – doing something outrageous is a tactic. A strategy is a long-term approach that the organization will use to get the message out and inspire people to raise money. Staff in an organization could simply get together and use a formal technique to generate a good idea. Any software that facilitates group brainstorming would be helpful to a geographically dispersed group of fundraisers.

Many localities have similar program and policy needs. Groups in different locations face similar challenges in selling their ideas, funding their programs, and getting the public's attention. Activist groups may also need to develop ballot initiatives and regulations that can sell. How will all of that happen? Collaboration across geographic boundaries and types of organization could help. Within an organization a dispersed group of volunteers and staff could collaborate using group brainstorming software. A crowdsourcing site devoted to activism in general or to creating and "selling" progressive social policies could be useful. Similarly, crowdsourcing could lead to new and better ideas for social service programs and public education efforts.

Different types of policy require different brainstorming efforts. Social issues, environmental issues, and economic problems call for different sorts of solutions. The different legal, cultural, political, and technological factors dictate that different sorts of policies be handled differently in both idea generation and the selling of the idea.

Many localities have similar program and policy needs. Groups in different locations face similar challenges in selling their ideas, funding their programs, and getting the public's attention. Activist groups may also need to develop ballot initiatives and regulations that can sell. How will all of that happen? Collaboration across geographic boundaries and types of organization could help. Within an organization a dispersed group of volunteers and staff could collaborate using group brainstorming software. A crowdsourcing site devoted to activism in general or to creating and "selling" progressive social policies could be useful. Similarly, crowdsourcing could lead to new and better ideas for social service programs and public education efforts.

12 – Two Comprehensive Strategies

Two comprehensive problem-solving strategies deserve detailed coverage here. Richard Fobes describes one comprehensive brainstorming strategy in *The Creative Problem Solver's Toolbox*. In *How to Think Like Einstein*, Scott Thorpe describes a formal problem-solving strategy based loosely on the thinking style of Albert Einstein. Some people might appreciate a complete pen-and-paper strategy for solving problems. Two of the best and their social betterment applications are introduced in this chapter. You will probably want to read one or both of the books, but this chapter contains enough detail to duplicate parts of each strategy.

A Problem-Solving Toolbox

Richard Fobes describes one strategy in his book *The Creative Problem Solver's Toolbox*. The strategy he prescribes follows a familiar pattern: Define your challenge, generate and evaluate ideas, refine your idea, decide whether to implement your idea. In Fobe's method, idea generation and idea evaluation go together. As ideas are generated they need to be evaluated for weaknesses (or disadvantages as Fobes often calls them) and refined. Ideas can also be combined with other ideas, in whole or in part, before critiquing and refinement occur. Deciding whether to implement your idea is a new subject.

We usually assume that if the idea will help and we have the resources then we should go ahead and implement the idea. Sometimes that's true and sometimes it isn't. The problem is that sometimes an idea can cause a worse problem than it solves. It is up to the "idea people" to make sure that an idea is unlikely to cause a bigger problem than it solves.

Trying to "sell" or implement a bad idea while covering up or ignoring a major downside is not going to work. People will see the problem coming and reject your idea. People may also react against your group and your cause because the idea is obviously going to cause another serious problem. Most people won't stand for that sort of thing and those are the same people who will decide if your idea works or not!

Any idea that would impose a significant hardship on many people to solve a problem that many people don't recognize or that they want to address in other ways is a sure prescription for: failure, wasted money, disillusioned staff and volunteers, and loss of credibility. That gas tax example is just an obvious illustration of what can happen when we become fixated on the "good" or "necessary" idea that hasn't been subjected to proper scrutiny.

What is proper scrutiny? It depends on the subject. If you want to buy a few new PCs for your nonprofit the decision to only consider Energy Star rated systems should be easy. Deciding to campaign for tough new "green" building standards statewide is something that needs to be evaluated much more thoroughly. Does the organization have the resources and skills available for such a lofty objective? Does this goal even mesh with citizens' interests? How can you make the idea more attractive to people, voters or politicians, or business owners?

Fobes describes many tools and techniques to apply in the quest for better ideas. Most of his advice can be presented as a six-step plan for generating workable ideas. Some chapters in the book focus on advanced tools that need to be studied in detail before they can be understood.   A description of each step follows this summary:

1. Get into a creative thinking mindset.

2. Define and refine your goals.

3. Generate some ideas.

4. Refine your idea.

5. Test your idea.

6. Decide whether or not to implement the idea.

Start the search for a great idea by adjusting your mindset using several techniques Fobes recommends. Decide to pursue an ideal solution. Even if you don't ever get there, the pursuit of an ideal solution will produce better thinking. Accept that most ideas will need some work; a perfectly formed idea is unlikely to spring straight from anyone's mind. Try different perspectives without judging any for their "rightness" or quality. Use your sense of humor. Humor breaks us out of habitual patterns of thinking. And write down your ideas! Don't assume they'll come back to you when needed because they probably won't.

The real creative work starts with defining and refining a goal. "A world free of poverty" is a desire not a goal. Establishing an innovative new poverty-reduction program for rural villagers in developing countries is a goal. There is a specific "product" and a suggestion of concrete actions to take. Depending on your experience level, you may need to start by volunteering at an international development charity or by reading books on how to start a nonprofit. Doing both would be even wiser. You'll need an idea that qualifies as innovative and practical. You'll need money and staff. Then, you'll need to get to work. You'll need interim objectives. Once the organization actually implements your program you'll want to have concrete goals in mind. Perhaps the idea is for local governments or nongovernmental organizations to duplicate your program. A goal might be to have the program duplicated by at least 15 organizations in five African nations in 3 years.

Before setting concrete goals it might be useful to step back and ask some goal-related questions. What do you really want to accomplish? Express your goal in positive terms. Negative goals don't motivate people as effectively. Make sure you are personally excited by the goal (advice from Scott Thorpe). Be willing to change goals at any time. Know whether you are pursuing a final goal on an interim goal that can lead you to something bigger. Try to pursue multiple, prioritized goals instead of having one thing in mind. Try "pulling" people by offering something positive rather than "pushing" people away from a certain behavior or attitude with the threat of being punished.

Fobes also points out that a goal can be pursued indirectly, using one or more of four approaches: amplification, leverage, redirection, and step-by-step. *Amplification* means to make your claims bigger (without being dishonest or ridiculous) or to make more noise or create bigger advertisements. *Leverage* is about finding a way to act that provides the most "bang for the buck." Reducing homeless might work better if we create programs to intervene early in the descent into homelessness where it is less time-consuming and expensive to help people get their lives back together. *Redirection* means changing the focus of an argument or debate so that the terms favor your goal.

After carefully considering your goal, you'll need to generate some ideas. Fobes' idea generating techniques are familiar enough. He recommends using combinations of existing ideas, concept fans, morphological analysis, and random input to generate ideas. He also recommends using evaluation along with idea generation rather than holding evaluation to the end. As ideas are generated people can always try to combine them, or strengthen them by identifying and removing one or more disadvantages.

Testing and Implementing an Idea

Once refined the idea needs to be tested before being implemented. This testing is one use for thought experiments or Consequence & Sequel. Fobes has additional suggestions for testing ideas. Fobes also describes thought experiments but adds the caveat that a thought experiment will only work if the experimenter is thoroughly familiar with the subject at hand. So, don't try thought experiments in areas that are well outside your areas of expertise. Imagine negative consequences. This is a different focus from simply thinking about what could go wrong. A dizzying array of things could go wrong when an idea is implemented. The specifics vary with the type of idea. It is always true that some things are highly improbably, or nearly certain, or escape the attention of the experimenter, or are too numerous and complicated to consider in a reasonable amount of time.

Fobes also advises that ideas be tested before full-scale implementation. An idea can be tested by breaking it into parts and testing the parts or by implementing the complete idea on a small scale. This is commonly known as a pilot project or a demonstration project. Dividing an idea into parts and testing the parts may be more difficult to manage with social betterment ideas.

No idea should be implemented without considering whether or not the idea should be implemented. Knowing the idea will really address the problem and advance a cause is not good enough. If the idea still has negative consequences that are not trivial (e.g., much more commuting time) then the idea should *not* be implemented. Exceptions are tolerable if the idea is designed to address a crisis or an imminent threat. An imminent threat here is one that is specific and has clearly understood consequences. Global climate change is not an imminent threat in this sense because the existence, types, and magnitudes of the likely problems are still in dispute.

When your idea is tested and ready to be implemented the only remaining step is to get busy! This is where some advanced and detailed planning comes into play. You should have already decided on a first action step and considered relevant factors in successful implementation – resources available, resources needed, fit with local social environment, and in some cases fit with the natural environment in some cases. Fobes suggests some additional questions to ask when preparing to implement any idea (from Fobes, pages 248-249):

1. Does it really solve the problem?
2. Does it solve the problem or just eliminate the symptoms?
3. Is it a temporary fix or a permanent solution?
4. Does it solve the whole problem or only part of the problem?
5. Is the solution simple or complex? (Simple is better.)
6. Are there disadvantages for people who are supposed to benefit?
7   Does the solution benefit nearly everyone or only a select few?
8. Are there potential problems that you hope people won't notice?
9. Are you comfortable with your answers to the these/questions?

If you are comfortable with your answers to that list of questions and there are no negative consequences of significance, then the idea is ready to use. Remember that a negative consequence is, or should be, an idea killer if the consequence is nontrivial and highly probable. A significant negative consequence of any sort should only be tolerated if there is really a dire need to implement the idea. Vaguely "urgent" problems like families living on the street or global climate change don't count. Those problem statements are too vague and general to suggest useful directions for creative work. What's needed is a specific statement of *why* families are living on the streets. Once the contributing factors are at least tentatively identified its possible to imagine some way of mitigating the conditions that lead families to live on the streets.

Einstein Thinking in Action

Some social problems are exceptionally vexing and persistent. Social programs and government policies seem to have limited impact except to use up plenty of time and money. These problems might be so tough because our approach is wrong, our commitment is insufficient, our knowledge is lacking, or intractable causes (like human nature) are the primary contributors. For purposes of this book, the correct answer doesn't matter. It seems that the correct assessment of the situation will vary with the specific problem in question. Continued gun violence may have more to do with human nature than with lack of knowledge about the problem and its proximate causes. Persistent poverty in the United States may have more to do with lack of knowledge of how biological, cultural, historical, and psychological factors interact. In the former case we are stuck with addressing symptoms of the problem or the proximate causes like liberal gun control laws.

Scott Thorpe wrote a book that describes an approach to problem solving that is loosely based on the thinking style of Albert Einstein. Thorpe's method is applicable to tricky social problems. Indeed, Thorpe applies the elements of his "Einstein method" to the problem of world hunger. While this problem may be too much for any one person or group to tackle regardless of their intelligence, creativity, and drive the Einstein method is still a viable approach to any social betterment problem.

Like any decent problem-solving method the Einstein method begins with defining the problem or problems. Thorpe directs readers to list the problems they are interested in solving. For practical reasons it may be best to start with one social betterment challenge and do three things: state the problem concisely, state why the problem must be solved, and state the next/first action step in solving the problem.

Important warning: The first step must be something concrete that you can actually do now or in the immediate future. It does no good to say that the first action step is getting people to care about the problem. What does one actually do with a thought like that? No concrete action suggests itself. If you intend to raise public concern about an issue to the level where people are inspired to take some concrete action you need to first do two things. First, decide what exactly you will do to start the process of convincing people to care about the issue. Second, you have to decide what you want people to do. You may want to reverse the order of those two steps. You'll also want to ask who your audience is, how you can reach the audience, and *what benefit you can offer them that they will care about without any need of convincing.*

Step two in the process begins with writing a concise, under 25 words, statement of the problem. Then you create a "problem hierarchy" describing the higher-level needs satisfied by a solution to the problem. Higher-level needs include things like contributing, belonging, and self-esteem. Decide whether or not this is the real problem and what sub-problems are parts of the larger problem. Identify the limitations that stand between you and a solution to the problem. The limits to consider include commitment, money, attitude, education, schedule, skill, ego, knowledge, money, fear, and red tape. Then identify three "standard" answers for this problem. You will deliberately ignore them and look for something new. Step two ends with a new, simplified statement of the problem. Try defining the problem in one phrase, such as "increasing solar power usage."

The third step in this process is to consider motivation. You will need something strong to keep you going any the face of the opposition and ridicule you are likely to encounter: "You mean to get 167 world leaders to sign an agreement to stop using land mines? That is just crazy!" Motivators can be carrots (positive things) or sticks (negative consequences) that come from the idea. At this point in the process you can consider shrinking or expanding the problem to encourage action. An idea can be shrunk or expanded in several ways. Increase or decrease the number of people affected or the geographic area affected or the number of behaviors or laws or policies affected. The last element in step three is to make sure you find this version of the problem compelling.

Step four is quite simple. Add your motivators and size changes to a revised and expanded problem statement. Now your problem statement will include a problem to solve, why to solve it, and where to solve it.

The sixth step in the Einstein method is a form of brainstorming. This brainstorming could technically be done using just about any method of generating ideas. Simple concentration on generating solutions to the problem, however crude and impractical they may be, is one possible brainstorming method. Thorpe recommends different versions of random input as well as a related technique that involves using alternate realities. Thorpe also suggests using several techniques to generate a many "idea seeds," crude ideas that will be combined or refined at a later point in the process.

In his method you could randomly be directed to think like Cleopatra or to think about how a food fight could produce a solution to the problem. Unfortunately, you need to know something about Cleopatra, or 18th century France, or your hometown in 1968 (another perspective that's identified in *How to Think Like Einstein*). Changing the parameters of a challenge can also lead to new ideas: Can you make the solution free, twice the current price, ten times as rewarding, a "win" for your opposition, something that doesn't punish anyone, or something that removes a hassle in peoples' lives. Pick any one of those parameter changes and see how it affects your thinking. (Other possibilities include time frame, geographic scale, audiences to target, and behaviors versus perceptions.) The hassle in question need not be related in any way to your real goal. A campaign to get more people to ride bicycles might remove the hassle of

_____.

Thorpe also describes new tools that we can use. His list, once again it is supposed to be used to randomly select a tool, includes yellow pages, a pocketknife, a press release, spit and bailing wire, change of heart, invisibility, a billboard, a smart dog, a song, and a famous aunt. Thorpe does define how each new tool could be used. Suffice it to say that the point is to determine how the problem could be solved (or would be solved) using the tool. What advice would your

famous and wise old aunt give you? How would you solve the problem
if your only resource were the yellow pages of the local phone book?
You could also roll a die to select a random marketing tool:

Dice Roll

1. *Sidewalk sale* - "How can a sidewalk sale "sell" veganism?
2. *Vending machine* - How can vending machines promote
   veganism?
3. *Christmas sale* - How can a Christmas sale reduce teen
   drinking?
4. *Free gift* - Can a free gift help use promote animal welfare
   laws?
5. *Free trial* - Can we help people experiment with vegan eating?
6. *Early-bird special* - Can you offer a bonus to people who act
   quickly?

Any other form of idea generation technique would work just
as well. Maybe you can reduce your problem to a list of problem
elements and characteristics, which makes the problem suitable to
morphological analysis. Anyway, the Einstein method requires us to
evaluate each idea by asking two hard questions: Why will this idea
work? Why will the idea *not* work? If you can't think of any reason
why an idea won't work, try harder.

Ideas may need to be combined with other ideas to create a
workable and improved idea. Thorpe offers several techniques we can
use to work with ideas to make them stronger. Each technique relies on
the idea "seed" created in the previous step.

The next stage in Thorpe's process could be performed at any time. You should identify the rules you operate by or that define a good idea. List all of the rules, principles, and assumptions that seem to have some bearing on creating a workable solution to your chosen problem. Play with these rules in one of five ways:

1. *Violate the rule* – note that this rule doesn't apply to laws, regulations, or moral principles.
2. *Circumvent the rule* – Is there a way to work around the rule and still solve the problem?
3. *Opposite rule* – Can the rule be reversed to yield a potential solution to the problem?
4. *Special case* – Can this instance be granted an exception to the rule?

Later in the Einstein method you will ask yourself the same questions about ideas that have come out of using the idea seeds created in step two.

Applications

Suppose you are interested in getting people to choose renewable energy sources over fossil fuels or nuclear energy. You've decided to focus on home energy use, so you want people to choose renewable energy sources to meet their electricity needs. The usual methods don't seem to be working; at least they aren't working quickly enough for you. What can you do about this situation? This is the sort of big, complex challenge for which the Einstein method is suited.

The problem-solving process starts with a statement of the problem you want to solve. The problem here is the slow adoption of renewable energy technologies for home power generation. For illustrative purposes I'm ignoring the practical differences between gas, electricity, and home heating oil. An idea solution would displace the last two and provide for heating and cooking with a renewable energy source.

Having made an initial problem statement you need to explore the reasons for attacking this particular problem. Concern over the impact of global climate change could be one good reason for attacking this problem. Concern over the health effects of continued heavy use of fossil fuels would be another plausible reason for our focus on renewable energy for the home. The other environmental impacts, such as water pollution and damage to forests, could also motivate us to try and sell greener alternatives to fossil fuels. Focusing on home energy needs is a perfectly legitimate way to narrow our focus.

You need to identify a next step in dealing with the problem. The next step needs to be something concrete and something that a small nonprofit could easily do. You might select an even narrower focus by choosing one technology to promote and one geographic area to promote it in. Several reasonable choices of technology exist, and all have their merits and demerits. Solar photovoltaic cells seem like a good choice. The geographic focus could be the Washington, DC area. The objective could be to get people to install photovoltaic panels on their homes.

This is a good time to stop and consider how our problem – slow adoption of renewable energy technologies for home energy production – fits into a hierarchy of problems. What higher-level need is being served by solving this problem? The higher-level need could be the need to protect society from the impacts of global climate change, by reducing greenhouse gas emissions. That higher level need could also be the foundation for other problem-solving efforts. For instance, we could try to promote dramatic improvements in energy conservation. We could try to promote more transit-oriented development where high-rise offices and apartment buildings surround mass transit stops. A second high-level problem could be the need for Washington DC to shift to a renewable energy economy. We could take that problem as our target and come up with other renewable energy goals to focus on. Or, the original goal of promoting solar photovoltaic use on homes could remain the focus. Considering the problem at different levels of abstraction can help us see new ways of reaching a goal. This process is the equivalent of Fobes advice to explore your goal to see if it is really the right goal to pursue. We've decided to stick with the simplified problem of slow adoption of renewable energy technologies by homeowners. Given that focus, what options can we generate for convincing people to use more solar photovoltaic technology?

Now comes the time for some serious creativity. We'll need to work with several sources of idea seeds. Then we'll need to examine the idea seeds for some workable ideas. Random input is one great source of idea seeds. We can get a random word/idea seed by opening a dictionary to a random page and picking the first noun. Suppose we do this and get "lizard" as our first idea seed. What characteristics or attributes does a lizard bring to mind? Lizards are cold-blooded and shed skin. Some lizards can break off their tails to distract predators. Most lizards are carnivores. Most boys seem to like lizards.

What if we only had one tool to help us solve our problem? What if we had Google, and only Google, to rely on as a problem-solving tool? How would we use Google to help us solve the problem? We could search for partners, either nonprofits or businesses. We could search for information on grants. We could search for research or case studies that could help us do a better sales job.

The characteristics of Google could also suggest a new approach to the problem. Google is obviously a search tool that people can use by entering a key word or phrase. Advertisers can buy sponsored listings that appear next to search results. Google has a specialized search feature that covers scholarly articles. There are also Google maps.

We should also consider different approaches to our problem by asking how other people might solve it. How would a missionary solve the problem of slow adoption of renewable energy sources for homes? Would he or she tell stories about how peoples' lives have changed because they embraced renewable energy technologies? Maybe the missionary would move into a cottage that has solar cells on the roof, to make his or life an example for others. The missionary would likely have literature to share with people who are interested in learning more about renewable energy options.

If conditions were different – social or political or economic – how could the problem be solved? Maybe full-cost pricing would solve the problem. The full environmental and health costs of relying on fossil fuels would fall on homeowners. What would people do in that situation? Does this situation suggest anything that might be done in real life to promote renewable energy technologies?

Everyone uses rules to think about things, how things are done, how they should be done, how they have to be done. These rules can be broken, or somehow worked around. Of course that observation doesn't apply to laws, regulations, or moral principles. What rules about home energy use are holding us back and how do we deal with those rules? Several rules suggest themselves:

1. Utilities supply electricity and most people like it that way.

2. Homeowners don't want to be hassled with solar power equipment.

3. People resist change because they are afraid of what could go wrong.

Other rules may well occur to the reader but the proceeding three are good enough for illustrative purposes.

How can each of those rules be ignored, circumvented, replaced by an opposite rule, violated, or set aside by making our solution a special case? We can violate the rule by telling people to make their own electricity, maybe. We can circumvent the second rule by telling people how easy it is to install and maintain solar PV panels (for do-it-yourself types). We can circumvent the third rule by focusing on people who've demonstrated in some way that they are especially open to change.

Rules aren't the only constraints on what we can do. Those constraints need to be identified and dealt with in some way, or we'll never come up with a breakthrough solution to the problem. Many possible constraints exist in a social betterment effort, but they usually fit in the categories of financial constraints, lack of knowledge, physical laws, legal restrictions, and customs and preferences. We can circumvent those constraints, violate them, ignore them, work with the opposite constraint, and treat our solution as a special case. Many constraints might affect our ability to get people to use solar panels on their homes.

1. *Financial* – many people lack the extra money, or think they

do.

2. *Lack of Knowledge* – people don't know how to select or install solar cells.

3. *Physical Laws* – there are no obvious constraints here.

4. *Legal Constraints* – ordinances and community bylaws may restrict how and where solar cell panels could be mounted on homes or apartment buildings.

5. *Custom & Preference* – convenience (a value) and the "ugliness" of solar panels (aesthetic sensibilities) are limits.

The financial constraint on solar PV use could be circumvented by identifying and publicizing grants people could use, or by publicizing the installation costs and utility savings for a typical home. The purchase and installation cost might be paid back more quickly than people think. The legal constraints could, potentially, be overcome by negotiating with homeowner associations and zoning boards to get solar PV panels treated as a special case, one immune to the usual restrictions on mounting things on the roof. Lack of knowledge is easy enough to overcome with a little public education. In principal at least, there are no "rules" or constraints that will stop us from solving our problem.

Now is the time to return to those idea seeds that we started to use before. What ideas are suggested by thinking like a missionary, considering the attributes of a lizard, and using Google as our only problem-solving tool?

What inconvenient facts does a winning idea need to account for? Answering that question is the next step in the Einstein method. Inconvenient facts can be circumvented, ignored, violated, invalidated by making our solution a special case, or turned into an opposite. Four possibilities and a coping strategy for each fact are as follows:

1. Solar panels are expensive (focus on energy savings from using the panels)
2. Management of the system takes extra time (ignore this)
3. Management needs new expertise (offer free maintenance and operations advice)
4. Sunlight varies widely in strength (stay hooked into the electrical grid)

Inconvenient facts 1, 2, and 4 suggest new elements to include in our target solution for the problem.

Specifying a target solution is the next stage in the Einstein method. Considering the original problem statement, some seed ideas, inconvenient rules, and some inconvenient constraints leads to a detailed solution. We will now focus on selling people on the idea of using state-of-the-art solar PV technology by distributing information on costs, operations, maintenance, and benefits to homeowners. The information will also include advice on operation and maintenance of power storage systems, on cutting the cost of purchasing and installing the systems, and information on "regular" people who are using solar panels to generate some of their own electricity. This is at least a good start on a really innovative solution to the problem of getting people to more quickly adopt renewable energy technology.

We may, and probably should, want to work with other people or talk to other people about our idea. Who? In this case we would want to talk with an experience advocate of renewable energy, and perhaps with someone who knows how to select, install, and maintain solar PV systems. Since we 值 1 probably need to convince certain homeowner 痴 associations or zoning boards to let people generate their own electricity, somebody who has experience in similar efforts would be someone to talk with. One of those people could even become a partner in this effort. We 壇 naturally want a partner who complements our own skills and personality. In the author 痴 case a partner who has experience with this sort of initiative and an outgoing personality would be highly desirable.

13 – Selling Social Change

Getting a good idea is only part of the problem-solving process. You may need to convince other people to go along with the idea so they will give you a grant! Giving some thought to how you can sell the idea to those who need to act on the idea is vital to the idea's success. This chapter offers observations on the selling of ideas through application of some thinking.

Lateral thinking tools such as AGO, FIP, and OPV are useful in the "selling" stage. Devising a clever and effective way to sell a new idea is also a good subject for lateral thinking, with an emphasis on provocation and concentration. Advertising and marketing techniques can always be applied to social betterment.

Advertising

Advertising is only one part of selling an idea, with marketing and public relations being the other two elements to consider. The important elements to consider in an advertising campaign are medium, message, and strategy. The medium is simply the media that will be used to advertise. The obvious and easy choices are newspaper ads, banner ads, and Web classifieds. Many other media are worth considering, especially for organizations with limited budgets. Distributing stacks of informational flyers in local businesses could work.

Make good use of the World Wide Web too. Create persuasive

and interesting pages on social media sites, including Facebook. Don't overlook smaller social networking sites like Orkut, Good.is, and Idealist.org. Use the sites to run small ads where that sort of marketing is allowed.

Giving out products like refrigerator magnets and ballpoint pens with a slogan and URL might help. Print/make lots of copies for distribution at in-person networking events, and special events like Earth Day. Create a small badge that people can download and put on their own site. Creating and sharing simple code is easy these days. An "I Love the Greene River!" badge with your organization's URL at the bottom can be a legitimate way to advertise the organization.

The audience is still the most important consideration in advertising. What do they read and where do they go? If they rarely use the Internet then, of course, online advertising is a waste of time and money. Where can this audience be reached? What medium works best for the audience? And what is the message you want them to get?

The advertising message could provide information or an inducement to take some action or think about something. In commercial advertising the goal is to get you to buy something. In social change advertising the goal is to teach people something new or get them to take a particular action, either for their own benefit or for the community. The same tools that advertisers and marketers use to sell goods and services can be put to use for social betterment,.

AGO

This lateral thinking technique should be used at the beginning of all social betterment efforts, including the selling of ideas. Take a few minutes to consider specific aims, goals, and objectives for your promotional effort, program, or organization. The distinctions between aims, goals, and objectives are not important. The point is to focus specifically on the sort of social change that you to accomplish.

Maybe some possibilities have to be ignored because of resource limitations or time limits or the current state of technology. Aiming to get a fuel cell in 200,000 Virginia homes by 2020 is a recipe for failure for even the largest and richest nonprofit. Why? Residential fuel cell technology is still immature, expensive, and not well understood by the public. There are no compelling advantages for homeowners relative to solar cells, diesel backup generators, or just relying on power from the electrical grid.

Copywriting

Copywriting is the art of writing to sell products, services, or ideas. A copywriter writes to get readers to take a specific action, ordering a free report from a Web site for example.

The same persuasive writing tools used to give away free reports on the internet, to sell insurance, and to peddle produce can also "sell" policies or programs. The basic principles of copy writing are not too difficult. A self-starter who likes independent learning could master the basics by reading one book and practicing.

Copywriting works in print media and in online media, in short advertising pieces and in eight-page letters. Web copy that solicits donations or sells a product or pitches attendance at a conference could be improved by applying some copy writing principles. Small newspaper ads with only a couple dozen words can be improved as well.

Like any form of writing, the art of writing effective copy does take some time to master. This should not dissuade anyone from picking up the basics and using them to create better ads, email messages, and Web content. Buy and use a guide book like *Web Copy That Sells* by Maria Veloso.

FIP

Thinking about priorities is always helpful when planning any social betterment activity. Planning to sell an idea is no exception. You'll want to think about the ideas that could sell, to whom and prioritize the list of possibilities.

Evaluate ideas in terms of impact relative to the investment of time and money. What idea would be reasonably easy to "sell" and would have a significant impact? If you want to advertise ways for people to reduce their meat consumption, what option is likely to reduce meat consumption the most? Now, do you have the resources to promote that idea, or one like it? This question should be the first one that comes after creation of a good idea to address that priority. Idea generation comes after definition of what counts as a good idea.

Guerrilla Marketing

The concept and term were invented by marketing guru J. Conrad Levinson and explained in his many books. Levinson wrote books on the general applications of guerrilla marketing and on applications to online marketing. The principles should be particularly useful tools in the hands of small nonprofits with tiny budgets. The basic idea behind guerrilla marketing is to use unconventional and low-cost marketing techniques to reach your audience.

Here are some principles of guerrilla marketing, adapted from the "guerrilla marketing" entry on Wikipedia:

1. It should be based on human psychology instead of experience, judgment, and guesswork.
2. Instead of money, the primary investments in marketing should be time, energy, and imagination.
3. Concentrate on how many new relationships are made each month.
4. Focus tightly on one message.
5. Instead of concentrating on getting new customers, aim for more referrals, more transactions with existing customers, and larger transactions.
6. Forget about the competition and concentrate more on cooperating with other groups and organizations.
7. Always use a combination of marketing methods for a campaign.
8. Use current technology as a tool to empower your marketing.

Go through that list and reflect for a few minutes on how to use each of the principles in your own marketing, fundraising, and advocacy efforts.

Logic Bubbles

An idea won't sell because it is a "good" one. An idea has to appeal to peoples' wants or needs and has to fit with their existing lifestyles. Selling an idea involves trying to get into a target individual's head. What does he or she think about the issue in question?

Given his or her knowledge of the issue and likely opinion, how will your idea be received? What elements may need to be changed or dropped to make the idea more marketable to the intended audience? Those questions apply to any sort of audience, powerful or not, rich or not, socially conscious or not.

Your own logic bubble is important, but probably a bit harder to see. What are your assumptions, beliefs, and perceptions about the issue? How do you think your own logic bubble affecting what you consider a good idea? How do you think your logic bubble is shaping the idea that you want to sell?

Selling people on using renewable energy requires an understanding of the logic bubbles of the audience(s). We need to consider the reasons why people don't, for example, choose to buy electricity from green energy producers. Lack of knowledge, lack of a green energy alternative in the area, and money may all be explanations. "Doesn't renewable energy cost more? I'm already on a tight budget so why pay more for supposedly "greener" power? That reaction shows that the cost of energy is being equated with the electric bill. We know this isn't true, that burning fossil fuels imposes environmental costs and health costs. But we need to address the financial costs of "greener" power by writing about the health costs and environmental costs.

Marketing Physics

Doug Hall invented this concept and described it in *Jump Start your Business Brain*. Marketing physics is built on three principles – overt benefit, real reason to believe, and a definite distinction – that must be marketed to prospective customers. An overt benefit is a specific thing that customers will get by using the product. Of course the benefit also has to be something they want. A good overt benefit can be concrete, such as a 30% reduction in heating bills, or abstract. The benefit can be large or small, such as a fresher-tasting mouth. The benefit needs to come with a real reason to believe your product or service can deliver the benefit needed: "Our gum contains real peppermint oil." The product or service also needs to be dramatically different in some way that matters to the audience. The breath-freshening gum could temporarily stain a tooth blue if a cavity is developing.

All three concepts apply equally well to social change. Use a marketing campaign to answer the key marketing questions:

- What benefit will people get from acting on your idea?
- Why should they believe your claim about the benefit?
- What is dramatically different about the idea you are selling to the audience?

Answer each question for each audience and use the answers in all of the usual advertising media. Make sure people who can sell the idea face-to-face know how to answer those questions so they can champion the idea.

Idea Champions

Malcom Gladwell's best-selling book *The Tipping Point* introduced two new concepts that should be on the ambitious social changer's mind. Gladwell defines a tipping point as a threshold or "point of critical mass" when a significant change occurs. Ideas can have tipping points, meaning that at some point in the idea's adoption the idea "takes off" in a society. Behaviors can also reach and pass a tipping point. Fair trade shopping used to be something for a few West-Coast liberals and a few other social activists. The habit of buying fair trade certified good whenever possible may grow slowly, then rapidly become normal shopping behavior.

Mavens are people who are wild about a product or service. Social innovations of all sorts can also have mavens, who spread the word about a great idea. Ever had a stranger start talking to you about God? That person was probably enthusiastic enough about his or her faith to be a maven. Vegans and vegetarians are sometimes pretty quick to tell people about the benefits of their adopted eating habits. The important point about mavens is that any decent idea will attract some, with or without your conscious effort. Find mavens and keep them enthusiastic about the idea because this will make it easier for an idea to catch on.

Viral Marketing

Viral marketing is the art of spreading an idea from person to person through free reports, free e-books, blog posts, podcasts, video posts, or just about any other media people can be tempted or encouraged to share. Emails and free reports were probably the first viral marketing tools. Marketers invited people to share the report or forward the email, along with the marketing message contained therein. Why not use a similar concept to sell social betterment?

Author Ralph Wilson lists six viral marketing principles on his Web site Wilsonweb.com:

1.   Give away products or services.

2.   Provide for an effortless transfer to others.

3.   Do something that scales easily, from small to very large.

4.   Exploit common behaviors and motivations.

5.   Use existing communications network.

6.   Take advantage of others' resources.

Videos and audio files that people can download and share would work quite well. Have you ever visited YouTube? Maybe you have access to the technical skills and artistic creativity it would take to produce a catchy video that you could post on YouTube and other video sharing sites. The same sort of thing could be done with podcasts. Create an interesting commentary or "newsy" piece that promotes your cause and provides some entertainment value.

Write an e-book and distribute it for free using Web sites. An e-book is just what the name suggests – an electronic book intended to be read on a computer. Most e-books are about sales or marketing, but most every topic from autobiographies to zoology has probably been addressed in one of the many e-books now in print. What would people interested in social betterment write about? Your tactical approach should be the same as with other e-book or report writers. Cover a topic that you already know people care about, be it saving money, making money, appealing to the opposite sex, career success, health, safety, or one of several other motivators. Whatever your social betterment objectives are, there is bound to be some way to turn related information into a free report or e-book that people will download.

How do you create an e-book or a downloadable report? Reports are easy, since all you need are a report in some common word processor format, or in PDF format, and a Web page with a download link on it. e-books could be created using desktop publishing software or they could be created by e-book creation software. Many free and inexpensive options are available, as a quick online search will reveal.

The point of viral marketing is to create a message that people will want to share through email or social networking sites. Viral marketing works best on the Internet where it is so easy to share things, but offline viral marketing can also work.

Offline viral marketing could take several forms. Organizations could give away things that contain a social marketing message. Mailings that people are encouraged to share with their neighbors would also work. Bumper stickers and other small stickers (for telephone poles, trash cans and such) could be cheaply printed and distributed to people who want to display them on their own cars or post them around town. Viral marketing that's done online or in the real world could work for activism, social programs, public education, social marketing, and advocacy for policies or legislation.

14 – Advanced Change Tools

This book emphasizes relatively simple strategies for brainstorming, planning, and problem solving. There will be some occasions when advanced techniques are helpful. When? The more variables involved, the more likely you will want to use an advanced technique. Variables can include symptoms, root causes, influencing factors, intervening factors, and characteristics of the social environment. Challenges that cut across the responsibilities of agencies and the interests of different sorts of nonprofits may call for advanced problem-solving techniques.

The tools are listed according to the stage of innovation where they are most applicable. Trend analysis and causal mapping are best suited for problem analysis. (Other tools) are best suited to generating ideas. (More tools) are designed for decision analysis. Finally, enterprise innovation management is a large-scale organizing scheme for a big organization's efforts.

If these advanced techniques aren't actually required to solve a problem they may be needed to sell an idea to others. This is sometimes the best approach to solving a problem or exploiting an opportunity. In other cases, as when new laws or policies seem necessary, there is no other choice but to create an idea that will sell. In some instances the techniques in this chapter can even reveal a way to move past barriers like the need for sweeping policy changes or voter passage of a controversial initiative.

Causal Flow Diagramming

Sometimes we need to work on understanding the source of a problem, the factors that affect the problem, and the way various factors interact to influence the problem condition in question. Causal Flow Diagramming is one tool we can use to understand a problem in detail. It is never enough to say that people are poor because they lack opportunities, or worse to say that economic injustice makes people poor. Causal flow diagramming can also help you understand how a social system works. A social system could be a school, a company, a community, or any other collection of people, laws, rules, and technologies.

Causal flow diagramming has five steps, some of which require a good deal of analysis and specialized knowledge to carry out correctly. Before beginning you will need to specify the system or problem you want to understand. The first step in causal flow diagramming is to identify the major factors involved in a problem, or in the way a social system works. Step two is to identify the causes and effects – what elements of the problem or system act on other elements. Step three is to identify each relationship from step two as direct or inverse. A direct relationship indicates that the cause and effect vary in the same direction. An inverse relationship means that the cause and effect vary in opposite directions. There is no need to aim for mathematical precision here, or to differentiate between the virtually unheard of relations that are perfectly direct or inverse relationships and those that are *roughly* direct or inverse. The fifth step in causal flow diagramming is to, well draw a diagram. Put each factor in a box and connect the boxes with arrows. Label the arrows to indicate whether the relationship is direct or inverse.

The last and most complicated step is to analyze the

relationships and determine which relationships form self-stabilizing feedback loops and which relationships create unstable feedback loops.

Feedback loops can be difficult to identify, and may take some sophisticated research. Still, the basic steps are not hard to understand and can be applied to many causal flow diagrams.

Theory of Inventive Problem Solving

Developed in Russia as a method of solving engineering problems, TRIZ ('trees", from the Russian for Theory of Inventive Problem Solving) has attracted interest as a tool for social innovation. Given the way that TRIZ was originally designed, a direct application to social innovation just doesn't seem possible. The principles of TRIZ come from two sources – successful inventions, trade-offs or contradictions inherent in engineering design. To be useful in social innovation, all 40 TRIZ principles need to be reinterpreted for use on non-technological problems.

One might also need to analyze thousands of successful programs, policies, activism strategies, and regulations to extract some specific design principles. TRIZ principles for social innovation might not apply to all domains anyway. Social change efforts might be so different from social marketing programs that different TRIZ principles are called for.

Examining some of the TRIZ principles site will clarify the nature of the challenge for anyone who wants to tackle the challenge of creating a social innovation version of TRIZ. The following list contains the first six TRIZ principles that were listed on www.triz40.com:

1. Segmentation

2. Taking Out

3. Local Quality

4. Asymmetry

5. Merging

6. Universality

On an initial inspection it is not entirely clear how those principles could apply to the social realm. Other principles are completely inapplicable outside of engineering. Principle 38 is to use strong oxidants, principle 39 is the use of an inert atmosphere, and principle 40 is use of composite materials.

A matrix listing 39 contradictions common to engineering design problems would need to be redesigned in some way to accommodate social betterment. The conventional version of TRIZ uses contradictions like strength versus energy use of moving object, area of moving object versus volume of moving object and complexity versus durability of a moving object. TRIZ guides uses in selecting principles to use in resolving the various contradictions inherent in engineering design. A social innovation version of TRIZ would need to offer similar guidance.

The social world is ruled by cultural, economic, legal, ecological, and political considerations that make social problem-solving far more complex than engineering. Psychology also plays a huge role in developing and adapting social innovations. Creating a process of social innovation, especially one that promises to ameliorate the ideological and psychological influences on social problem solving, might actually be an honest revolution.

Contradictions exist in all parts of social life. In engineering there are conflicts between design goals, such as strength versus weight and cost versus performance. In designing social innovations, social programs, or social policies other contradictions need to be considered in developing a good solution. People don't want higher taxes, at least on themselves, but they do want excellent government services.

Many possible contradictions could be relevant to social change efforts. A partial list follows:

1. Time vs. money
2. Effectiveness vs. efficiency
3. Speed vs. quality
4. Outcomes vs. outputs
5. Breadth vs. depth
6. Democratic vs. elitist
7. Incremental vs. radical
8. Process vs. technology
9. Top-down vs. bottom-up

How could each pair of contradictions be used in social innovation?

Time versus money is one of the most familiar tradeoffs in life. How much money do we want to spend versus how much time do we have? A shortage of time can be made up for using money, e.g. by hiring more people. Money can be made up for with a slower and more leisurely approach. You probably can't do some things you'd like to do on time and for the money you realistically expect to have available. This is what is meant by the "time vs. money" contradiction.

Effectiveness and efficiency are two mutually exclusive goals, in general. One can have a maximally effective program or one that makes the best possible use of available resources, including people, facilities, and money. It is realistic to maximize both effectiveness and efficiency in some cases, but not most. You will need to choice whether to solve as many peoples' problems as possible or to give some help to the maximum number of people your resources permit.

Speed and quality are almost always mutually exclusive. Project managers have a saying: "You can have it done right, on time, on budget. Pick any two." The same equation often applies in policy and program planning. Can you do what you want, as you want it, in the time available, and with the money that's available? In most cases we are really talking about money that will be available, unless something else comes up. Administrations change and so do their priorities. An unforeseen budget crunch may derail a nonprofit organization's program. To get anything done in a timely manner may require accepting a lower level of performance than you had originally hoped for. We may need to be content with a one-year reduction of 20% in the number of middle-school students who try tobacco products for the first time. A program where this result was realistic is all that could be put together in the time available. With more money and more time perhaps to show results the program may have achieved a higher level of success, maybe a 50% reduction in three years.

Breadth versus depth is another generic tradeoff that many organizations need to make. Most companies tend to opt for breadth – a wide variety of product offerings. Some companies try to meet the needs of all types of customers for a particular service or product. Some companies sell cheap cars and very expensive cars, Toyota being one example with its Lexus brand of luxury cars.

Some organizations focus on one need that a variety of people have. Soup kitchens serve all homeless people of all types. Another organization may focus on providing a range of counseling, medical, and vocational services for homeless veterans. A few organizations can afford to run a soup kitchen, and a shelter, and a health clinic, and a substance abuse counseling program. Most organizations need to focus on doing one thing for a broad audience or doing many things for a narrowly defined niche.

Should the organization, program, project, or policy be run by the people affected or by a professional staff? It is possible for professionals to be in charge at one level and the clients or citizens at another. In most cases there will need to be a focus on one or the other. In some countries there are self-help groups organized by a nonprofit but run by the members, perhaps with guidance from a professional mentor or facilitator. This is a democratic organization. An economic development group where people receive advice from experts and participate in programs developed by those experts would be an elitist organization, though not in the pejorative sense of the word. This is the case even if the organization gets considerable information and advice from the locals. It may be possible to combine democratic and elitist governance models. A professionally run training program could prepare residents of poor rural villages to teach basic hygiene and sanitation practices to villagers. These local teachers are free to spread the information and manage their own time. This organization would be essentially elitist, in that there is no direct local input into decisions, but democratic in the sense that the people affected are put in charge of their own fates after getting some orientation and formal training.

What degree of change is there going to be, if your plan works? The obvious choices are radical change and incremental change. We can try to convince 100,000,000 people in the United States to become vegetarians over the next five years. Or, in five years we can convince a few million people to drastically reduce their meat consumption. Incremental changes are most often the only realistic choice. Some specific behaviors may be amenable to rapid change in a few years, but these situations are extremely rare. Try to name one rapid and substantial change (say 5 or 6 years) that doesn't relate to consumer goods and services.

A change effort can be multifaceted or conducted in stages. A broad plan can call for radical change over the long term, with many incremental changes along the way. This is certainly the most logical route to take in a grand vision of changing society. A staged approach to change just takes some elementary goal setting and planning: What exactly is the big change you desire? What steps will it take to make that change happen? In what order to the steps need to happen? How much time, money, and labor are required at each step? What is your target audience, or is there more than one target audience? How do you know who to target and how to target them? Does step X call for changing perceptions (how people think about a subject), behaviors, laws, or regulations? By and large, we can forget about changing peoples' beliefs and worldviews in the short term or medium term. The objective should be to change a behavior, get people to adopt a behavior, or get people to take a certain action. The desired action could be something that's done once (donate $30 to our cause) or repeatedly (take your recyclables to the curb every Wednesday night).

One part of a change effort could be radical while another could be incremental. This is a challenging but potentially powerful strategy. Consider gun control. You might want the city government to ban private ownership of handguns. This is certainly a radical change in most American cities! A less radical aspect of the same plan – to reduce handgun violence – would be to work with police to implement a gun buy-back program focused on handguns. Anyone can turn in a handgun and get some amount of money with no questions asked.

Finally, a change project can focus on social innovation or on technology. One organization probably lacks the resources to do both well. A social innovation is a process, organization, group, or action that's designed to address some social problem, or an opportunity. Technology is any application of knowledge to practical ends, so a new science-based form of psychotherapy is a technology. Blogs are a technology. Fuel cells are a technology. This latter meaning of technology -- hardware, software, tools, and combinations of the three -- is used here. As sociologist William Ogburne observed in the 1930s technology tends to change faster than other elements of society. If technological change is at all relevant to your cause, this may be a good place to start.

Merely substituting technology for something more difficult is probably a bad idea. To encourage obese person to take diet drugs instead of pursuing a healthy lifestyle is not a good idea. Nonprofits and local governments are pursuing the right strategy by using educational materials and advertising instead of giving away free diet drugs. Substituting Internet technologies for face-to-face communication and relationships is probably not something to encourage either. When should you focus on technology rather than process changes or other cultural changes? When technology is part of the problem or offers a quick solution to an urgent problem a technological solution makes the most sense. Consider fossil fuel consumption in the United States. It might be wonderful if people could be convinced to rely on public transportation or bicycles and live in apartment buildings and not single-family homes. Realistically that isn't going to happen in the near future. People might be convinced to buy "green" electricity from wind or solar power plants. They just need to know how to do it and how much it will cost. Those renewable energy technologies are a readily available way of reducing fossil fuel consumption. Big changes in American lifestyles may be required in the long run, but drastic short-term cultural change tends not to happen. When it does happen, the results probably won't be pretty. Consider forced collectivization and internal migration in the Soviet Union or China's Great Leap Forward. All three of those rapid and dramatic culture changes were massive human tragedies.

Other contradictions, or trade-offs as they could be called, probably exist. Some will be general sorts of contradictions similar to time versus money. Other contradictions will be particular to advocacy, education, fundraising, program design, social policy, and social services. The examples discussed in this section should make it easier to discern what those other contradictions might be. Once the contradictions are clear, it will be easier to decide how to engineer tradeoffs between one thing and the other. Making informed and carefully considered tradeoffs should increase the quality of ideas that get implemented.

Simulations

Simulations are mathematical models or computer programs that, well, simulate what happens in a social system, organization, culture, and so forth. SimCity is one popular and educational form of simulation software. Using simulations to evaluate the likely impacts of policies or legislation or regulations or programs would make for better planning. However, and this is a very important condition, the right variables need to be used in the simulation. The variables and their interactions have to be reflect reality to as great an extent as possible or the simulation will be wildly inaccurate and unreliable, perhaps disastrously so.

Running simulations is something best suited to a large organization or any size organization faced with a decision that can have huge impacts. In other cases, such as a community group planning to advocate a specific ordinance a thought experiment is a good substitute for simulations. Does the outcome of the thought experiment suggest that the proposed ordinance is really a good idea?

Decision-Event Tree

Sometimes the likely consequences of a decision need to be worked out systematically. One way of doing that is to construct a decision-event tree. This tree will form a chart that begins with the decision to be made, then lists each option, and the consequence(s) of choosing each option. If each decision would require making another decision then there is another level to the decision-event tree. There could be a series of events and choices involved in implementing a course of action, and this is where a decision-event tree can be useful in organizing your thinking. The decision event tree has several benefits:

1. Beaks the potential outcomes of a decision into a set of exhaustive and mutually exclusive branches.
2. Beaks possible scenarios into a sequence of events that can be easily compared.
3. My help to reveal new alternatives, and so is also a creative-problem-solving tool.
4. It helps you see how decisions and events are dependent on each other.

A decision event tree is usually a graphical tool, not one that's done purely by listing decisions and the likely outcomes. Represent those decisions and outcomes graphically by drawing a small square at the left edge of a piece of paper. Write the decision to be made in this square. Draw one line out to the right for each option you have at this point. Label each line with a word or phrase that summarizes the option. Consider the result of choosing each option and put that outcome statement at the end of a line that branches from the line you used to represent the option. Repeat this exercise for each of the options. Examine your growing tree for any options or results that may have been overlooked before. The next step is to estimate the probability of each outcome. For the purposes of constructing a decision tree, a general guess, like "20%," is good enough. The total odds of the likely outcomes for each option must total 100%. So, if one of our estimates is 20% and there are two other possible results of a choice then the other options would be assigned percentages that make the three total 100%. The point here is to exhaust all reasonably plausible outcomes of each choice, so forcing the total odds to total 100 is reasonable.

Step three in constructing a decision-event tree is the assignment of some output measurement to each option. This is usually a dollar value of goods or services sold. The social betterment world could use funds raised, petition signatures secured, percent increase in desirable behavior X, or percentage decline in undesirable behavior Y. That list is just meant to suggest many of the possibilities.

The final step in this process is to multiply each result's probability by the output of choosing that option. If result 5 has a 10% chance of happening and a value of $60,000, then the value of that option is $6,000. Now we have a quantitative basis for comparing one possible choice with the others.

A few words of warning: Steps three and four only work if there is some basis for calculating outcomes in the same way for all of your options. This is why the tool works so well in business where the outcomes of decisions can be measured in dollars. As the example below will indicate, many social betterment decisions don't have outcomes with such readily measured and compared outputs. In such cases you will have to make it a separate task to examine the value of each result. It might be easy to compare a 10% chance of getting a $60,000 grant to a 50% chance of raising $50,000 by direct mail and telephone calls. How do you compare a successful ballot initiative to getting 4 of 8 organizations to partner with you in projects to increase their use of renewable energy sources?

You may want to promote a certain cause or change but you can see many options for making progress. What should you do and what are the likely results? This is why a decision-event true can be useful. The tree lays out how the decisions and events can play out, perhaps revealing unexpected problems or opportunities.

A brief social change example will clarify the use of decision-event trees. The challenge before us is deciding how to best promote renewable energy use in the city. Assume we can choose each of the three available options:

1. Petition for a ballot initiative that requires city-owned vehicles to run on renewable energy sources. (A fuel like E85 does contain gasoline but would be allowed anyway.)

2. Creating newspaper ads that focus on simple, concrete steps people can take to buy renewable energy, such as buying "green" electricity.

3. Lobbying decision-makers at colleges and universities to use more renewable energy technologies and buy more "green" energy.

We would draw a little square and label it "renewable energy," then draw three lines spreading out to the right. The lines would be labeled "ballot initiative," "ads," and "lobbying." The likely results for each option are as follows:

1. Petition – success (added to ballot) or failure
2. Ads – success (increased purchasing of green energy), no effect
3. Lobbying – full success (all schools adopt our suggestion), partial success (some schools adopt our suggestion), or failure.

Next we need to realistically assess the probabilities of each outcome. For the petition, we might conclude that there is a 30% chance of success and a 70% chance of failure. What would success mean, in measurable terms? The obvious point is to get the ballot initiative passed so it is now a law, and not just a good idea. So, the petition option has another pair of outcomes to consider: passage or failure to pass. Passage may be good enough as a measure of success here. Call the percentage chance of success 40% and of failure 60%. Now there are two events standing between our choice to focus on that petition and the passage of a ballot initiative aimed at promoting renewable energy use. The prospects for this option do not look good: 30% (getting the proposal on the ballot) X 40% (odds of passage) = 12%. There is an 88% chance that the petition drive will fail or that the ballot initiative will be defeated.

We would repeat this exercise for all options and their results. Then we could make a better-informed decision about how to best use our limited resources. We might survey people to see if those newspaper ads have any effect on their energy decisions. The number of people who say they took a particular action or actions will give us an indicator of success. We could assign two percentages to the outcomes, even though there are obviously many possibilities here: people don't do anything, a few percent do something, a sizable minority of the population does something, and so forth. For our purposes it is enough to be able to say that the ads had a measurable impact or they did not. Maybe there is a 40% chance of the ads having a measurable impact, and a 60% chance of nothing happening.

In cases like this one, with two outcomes that are defined in qualitative terms, you should try to capture the value of that outcome in some way. In the private sector we would want to apply dollar values to the various outcomes. What is the likely *net* gain from our spending on a newspaper ad campaign?   The ad campaign might, for example, cost $4,000 with a 50% chance of meeting a target of 2,000 new customers. If each new customer will generate $20 net profit the newspaper advertising campaign is worth $16,000 ($40,000 X 0.5 = $20,000, $20,000 - $4,000 = $16,000). Unfortunately, many social goals defy easy measurement in financial terms. Getting an idea on a ballot and then passed by voters marks two qualitative victories, but those outcomes can't be readily measured. The negative impacts – costs and labor hours – can usually be measured though.

This problem of negative impacts being easier to measure than the positive impacts is a serious problem for social betterment efforts. There are tow possible ways of addressing this measurement problem. One is to focus in estimating the number of positive outcomes: "This program will keep 4,000 at-risk teens from dropping out in the first two years." More education translates to more income, on average. The difference between what 4,000 high school dropouts could earn in X years compared to the amount 4,000 high school graduates would earn gives one crude measure of that program's impact. Assuming you can produce these sorts of numbers and back them up with authoritative sources for your facts or calculations, the financial benefits could be a good selling point for an idea.

Delphi Polling

This forecasting technique is typically used to study trends in technology, but trends in popular culture or social changes of any sort could also be addressed through Delphi polling. The technique, by the way, is named for the famous Oracle at Delphi who prominent Greeks often consulted before making important decisions.

The basic technique is not hard to understand. A group of experts, and it could be a very large group, is asked to complete a questionnaire on the probability of certain changes or events happening in some specific time period. The results are compiled and shared with the experts, who can then revise their original answers. This re-evaluation should yield better estimates of the probabilities of certain events, and the time frame when the events are likely to occur. A Delphi poll could produce a prediction that by 2030 the first commercial fusion reactor will be operating. This prediction means that, according to the experts polled, there is some percentage change (typically 50%) that the event will happen.

In social change, a Delphi poll could be useful in planning and advocacy. The research could be used in public education or in advocacy to promote a certain policy, program, or piece of legislation: "Research shows that by 2015, _____. Therefore we should _____." Delphi polling could reveal new and useful details about events related to lifestyles, values, environmental quality, crime, buying habits, families, work, health, or personal finance. One or more of those subjects is of interest to anyone interested in promoting social change or in improving society in some way. So, perhaps consulting with a research organization about a Delphi poll is a good idea. Like so many other advanced tools, this one is really best suited to a large organization.

Anyone could benefit from reviewing existing Delphi poll results. George Washington University and _____ have both conducted Delphi polls on technological trends. Consider using existing poll results as advocacy tools or in public education. Use the results to search for threats and opportunities that are relevant to your cause or to your organization. Look at the results as opportunities to better understand social problems and as opportunities to engage in some creative thinking. How can a policy or program address a particular event, either making it more likely or less likely or making it happen sooner?

Trend Analysis

Trend analysis is a planning tool and a decision making tool. What is likely to happen in the near future? What decisions do we need to make regarding our goals and objectives? Does anything that's developing pose a threat or offer an opportunity? What can be done now? That last question offers opportunities for creative thinking and for decision thinking. Something, an innovative education program perhaps, could be designed to address the problem or opportunity.

Conducting a trend analysis is much more complicated that interpreting the results of one that's already been conducted. Using trend analysis data should be part of every organization's planning and environmental scanning activities. Even an informal scan of trends within the organization or in the social environment can help you make better decisions about deploying resources. An informal trend analysis uses personal experience (checked against some facts please!), news stories, and existing statistics to answer questions. Going into a trend analysis with specific questions to answer is always better than just casting about for something interesting. A nonprofit concerned with teaching classes on computer software or job hunting might need to keep abreast of changes in the local economy, changes in information technology, trends in corporate applications of information technology, and trends in the population they serve. This can be done informally by doing surveys of students, by analyzing class enrollment statistics, by paying close attention to business and technology news, and by studying demographic statistics for the area.

Scenarios

Businesses and government agencies sometimes use scenarios to help them understand what might happen in the future. The point is not to predict the future but to decide what elements of the future social environment. Being able to construct a range of realistic possibilities helps managers to position the organization for future success. Whole books have been written on constructing and using scenarios so it would be pointless to explain the process in a few paragraphs.

Nonprofit staff and social entrepreneurs will find many uses for scenarios. For example, what will a proposed riverfront development project do for quality of life in the community? A well-thought out scenario will demonstrate to skeptics why the idea is a bad one. Conversely, a scenario might make the development seem like a good idea.

Enterprise Innovation Management

Enterprise innovation management is a fancy term for a process any large, geographically distributed group or organization might do: set up a system to "manage" creation and implementation of new ideas. While it is true that creativity and inventiveness can't really be managed, the efforts of staff or volunteers, or both *can* be directed certain ways. Several specific creative goals could be managed at one time. The system could always be used to collect new ideas in other areas.

An activist group could establish as one its specific campaigns a call for new ideas about fighting global poverty. Individuals who develop or implement new ideas on their own could be promised recognition or some other symbolic award. Many people want to do something new, if not something "big," so they will be happy to have some direction for their creative energies. Anybody can be creative, especially with a little training in how to generate and refine ideas.

Not surprisingly, there is software available for enterprise innovation management, and there are consultants. A very large and geographically dispersed organization might need dedicated enterprise-level software and some technical advice. Most organizations will not need this much help.

Here is a simple method of enterprise innovation management.

It can be used in organizations of just about any scope and requires only slightly above average computer skills. Set up password-protected discussion groups, possibly using Yahoo! Groups, one for each area of interest. There should also be discussions devoted to fundraising, marketing the organization's programs, and perhaps one to stretching the organization's budget. People can review and comment on ideas. A moderator can review the ongoing discussions looking for ideas to implement. The other part of innovation management is overseeing the actual implementation of an idea. Perhaps the idea in question is a small one and won't cause chaos if it doesn't work out. In that situation innovation management amounts to taking whatever management steps are required to implement the idea, then monitoring the results. A bigger idea would be evaluated for potential risk and benefit, as well as for actual fit with the social environment. This is something that calls for professional training or an outside consultant.

15 - Assembling the Pieces

Creating change in society requires a comprehensive approach to diagnosing problems, asking questions, generating ideas, implementing ideas, selling ideas, and solving implementation problems. We also need to plan ahead and stay alert for opportunities or problems that are coming our way. Each of those processes has a place in social betterment work, though the ideal level of complexity is naturally going to vary. The higher the stakes the more rigorous the process needs to be.

A good strategy for social betterment includes all of the eight

1. *Analyze Challenges* – question assumptions and ask plenty of questions

2. *Plan Strategically* – the social environment, goals, and objectives need to be considered

3. *Steal Ideas* – look at many sources of information and ideas for anything you can use

4. *Think Design* – values, economics, social context) technology, economics, organizations, politics) influence what counts as a good design

5. *Think Creatively* –use brainstorming techniques or systematic idea generation methods

6. *Think Scientifically* – remember facts, theory, and logic

7. *Think Analytically* – test hypotheses, relate parts of the problem/issue to the whole

8. *Think Marketing* – audience, selling points, advertising media

Any group or organization can follow all of the steps in some way. Problem need to be analyzed to discover, if possible, the source or sources. Then we are in a good position to decide if we can solve the real problem or attack one or more of the symptoms. You might focus on getting groups with more power   to solve the problem. Knowing what counts as a good idea seems like an obvious step in problem solving. An explicit listing of the criteria might help you to think more clearly about ideas that come up later in the problem-solving process. In fact "write things down" should probably be added to that list of activism principles in Chapter One:

1. targeted innovation,

2. leverage,

3. empirical approach,

4. formalism,

5. marketing mindset, and

6. writing things down.

Asking good questions is always a sensible place to start when addressing any social change challenge or social betterment opportunity. Questions clarify objectives and evaluation criteria. Questions help to pinpoint the cause(s) of a problem and the characteristics of a good solution to the problem. Questions help people in social betterment work to better understand the social environment.

Brainstorming using pen-and-paper techniques or software needs to be employed to help exploit opportunities, improve things that are working now, and creatively solve problems. Some problems are amenable to conventional solutions. Those conventional solutions may still need some creative modifications to work in new circumstances. Most people only need to learn two or three brainstorming techniques to use. One relatively easy type of software is usually going to be enough. Computer savvy people will find it worthwhile to look at relatively complicated software like ThoughtOffice®.

Be a Better Activist

Here is a specific set of steps you could follow to solve a problem, improve something, or exploit an opportunity:

1. Create worksheets containing questions about your

challenge.

2. Learn two brainstorming tools.

3. Know what design values apply to your area of interest.

4. Learn an analytical problem solving technique, and use it.

5. Set up a system for environmental scanning.

6. Get training in problem solving or brainstorming.

7. Buy brainstorming software and start using it.

8. Master two idea evaluation methods, such as PMI and PCF.

9. Learn and use one decision analysis strategy.

Practice those evaluation strategies using the ideas listed in Appendix 2.

How much work will it really take to implement an innovation strategy? The time investment depends on how many of those checklist items you decide to implement. Setting up an environmental scanning system could take 40 person hours. Doing the scanning could take two or three hours a week. Implementing an idea management system could take 30-40 person hours for selection and procurement, if you are lucky. Doing everything else on the list less buying and learning that comprehensive problem-solving software may take 35-40 hours.

Implementing a crowdsourcing solution may only take 20-30 hours, plus a few hours a week during each idea generating campaign. Administration time should be similar for idea management software.

Mastering the individual techniques should take two or three hours for simpler techniques like PMI and random input or double that for the relatively complicated problem-solving tools like morphological analysis, problem analysis, and thought experiments.

Questioning Strategies

Asking questions could and should be part of each element of innovation strategy. At the goal setting stage there are questions about goals, objectives, problems, and symptoms. In setting the criteria for a good idea there are questions about the characteristics that a good idea needs to possess. Brainstorming often calls for asking questions to explore the nature of a challenge. Problem analysis needs questions about the nature of the problem. Decision analysis calls for answering some questions about the alternatives: What criteria should we use to decide what to do? Selling an idea to the board of trustees, voters, potential clients, or potential donors means asking some questions about the audience and their needs.

A serious innovation strategy requires knowing what sorts of questions to ask at what stage of the process. Some questions are harder to answer than others. Innovators need to know how to get the data or expert opinions that are needed for those tough questions. Review the types of questions that need to be asked at each stage of the process:

- When defining a challenge
- When deciding how to evaluate ideas
- When trying to diagnose a problem
- For solving a problem
- When designing a solution
- When trying to sell an idea to anyone
- When making a decision about some innovation
- When trying to improve an existing idea

You'll probably do it anyway. Make a plan to do it. Decide on the best locations for stealing ideas. Hit the bookstores, malls, and libraries. Take another peek at books and magazines you haven't read in some time. Watch different TV shows and read different magazines. Start out with knowledge of the areas in which you need to steal ideas. Consider management, advertising, financial management, fundraising, recruiting, retention, technology, volunteer management, strategic planning, social marketing, and anything else you can think of that's relevant to your organization.

Know your objectives! That will further focus your search for ideas worth stealing. Ideas aren't the only thing you can steal, or at least borrow for as long as needed. How would someone like that think about your challenge? What concepts and ideas can you take from this other person and use in your organization? You've already read about some sources of ideas. Here is some more general advice:

1. Read a nonfiction book that's way out your normal field(s).
2. Read different magazines with the same objective.
3. Surf Web sites devoted to topics that are new to you.

History, geography, physics, chemistry, ecology, sociology, psychology, engineering, and economics all offer the possibility of new ideas.

Don't work alone either! Enlist research assistants, friends in other organizations, or anyone you can find to help you find ideas and refine them or adapt them. Talk to other people and borrow *their* ideas.

Make a list of problems both large and small that your group or organization is facing. This list should include the main problem(s) for which your group or organization was created. The list should include any sub-problems of the main problems. Consult with coworkers on what needs to be on the list and on the wording that's been used. You will need this information for problem analysis and for group problem-solving sessions that may come later. Review the sections of Chapter 15 on action groups and creative hit lists. Review the problem analysis methods that are available and decide which one or two you want to learn more about and apply to these problems. Get some practice by starting with a relatively easy problem; even one that doesn't really seem to call for a formal problem solving process.

Practice with new problem-solving tools. Many are quite complex but some are probably going to be helpful, in spite of their complexity. Here are some sources of more information on problem analysis tools and their applications. More details on a few of the tools can be found in Chapter 4:

1. Chronologies
2. Causal flow diagramming
3. Hypothesis testing
4. Devil's Advocacy

Teach yourself how to use these tools by using exercises in *The Thinkers Toolkit* or by applying them to one or more problems that you've already identified. You did make that list of problems already, didn't you?

Brainstorming Techniques

Define a problem area where you want new ideas. Define an area where you want to exploit an opportunity and need a new idea. Pick a technique or two and apply it. The nature of challenges facing your organization will dictate, to some degree, the best choice of brainstorming tools. Refining an idea is different from defining a new creative focus and looking for an idea. Practice defining a new focus, a new symptom, or a new concept to brainstorm about.

Brainstorming Software

Decide what you need, how much you can spend, and who needs the software. Do you need only creative thinking software or software like ThoughtOffice(r) that offers comprehensive idea generation and problem solving tools? How many hours can you devote to learning new software? How computer-savvy are you? The more powerful the software the more time is probably needed to master it.

Focus on free software or software that can be used for free on a trial basis. There are several mind mapping options available in late 2013:

1. NovaMind® 3.2
2. FreeMind 0.8
3. Inspiration 8
4. MINDMAP Pro 4
5. BrainMine Standard 2005

More detail on all of this software is available at innovationtools.com. Since software comes and goes, or changes names, it doesn't make much sense to offer pages and pages of details here.

Decide what you want to do? Maybe some help in generating ideas is all that's really needed. If so then there is no need to bother with comprehensive problem-solving software. Even if new ideas are all that's needed, mind mapping software is still something to consider. Mind mapping itself takes a little effort to learn, but the software is not too challenging once those mind mapping principles have been mastered. Consider your resources, and the scope of the social change effort you are involved in. The more complex the subject matter, the more likely it is that you and some of your coworkers could get some value from comprehensive software like ThoughtOffice(r)® or MindSightss(r)®. So, the first step is to decide whether any complex desktop software is even necessary. The next step is to decide what exactly you want the software to do. This question could be investigated along with some investigation of the software packages that are available. Chuck Frey's Web site, Innovation Tools, offers the best starting point for investigation of problem-solving and brainstorming software. His site even has a whole section devoted to mind mapping.

Design Thinking

Consider the areas, techniques and values that relate to your organization's goals. What programs, policies, projects, or internal processes need to be designed or redesigned? Social innovations in general need to be designed deliberately rather than in a haphazard manner – This should exist so let's create it. Reviewing Chapter 8 on design thinking should lead to easy identification of the design operations that need to be used to improve the policy, program, project, or process in question. Design values need to be considered first, and formally. Don't forget to consider fit with the culture and with social values such as equity and democratic involvement.

Design Values

Consider the design values that apply to your organization's work, or planned work. How good is the fit? What redesign might be required? Especially consider the areas where your work may not fit so well with the social environment. Over the long term you may be able to change the social environment somewhat. If not, then what is the point of social services, public education, or activism? Design values considered before a project starts will, of course, help to create a more effective design or one that is easier to "sell" to people. Design operations are also important in the operational stage of a program or project. What needs to be done now to make our work more effective? What operations need to be carried out now? For existing programs or projects and new ones, design operations should be connected directly to the design values that are most relevant in a particular case. Design operations exist to support effective realization of the design values you previously identified.

Decision Analysis

What sorts of decisions will need to be made as the

organization's plans progress, as the program continues, as the policy is implemented? What sorts of decisions regarding fundraising, budgeting, staffing, and volunteer recruitment need to be made? Decision analysis usually hinges on gathering data or opinions. What data and (informed!) opinions will need to be collected so sound decisions are made? Where will that information come from?

In many cases, you will find that simple concentration on the pros and cons of each choice will suggest the right decision. Answering a question with a simple yes or no is sometimes easy and requires only the data and experience you already have at hand. In other cases some formal decision analysis tool will be needed. Likewise, prioritizing several options can be a seat-of-the-pants exercise or something that's proceeding with more formally, by rankings or comparisons among paired alternatives.

You'll want to start by determining where complex decisions are going to be called for. Study one or two decision-analysis tools so that you can use them with speed and confidence. This is also a good opportunity to look at comprehensive problem-solving software like ThoughtOffice®.

Collaboration

The first question is obvious: Do you need to collaborate with anyone outside of your current group, office, or organization? Knowing who those people are and where they are will help you determine what medium is best used. Maybe regularly scheduled meetings combined and conference calls are all the collaboration "tools" you need. Maybe you do need to use collaboration software. Idea management software might also be useful for a complex mission and a geographically dispersed group. You can get some benefits of idea management software by using collaboration software – specifically the ability to set up campaigns, allow interaction between members, and facilitate idea evaluation by one or more "judges."

The critical question to consider when starting out is the complexity of the task at hand, in terms of numbers of people and locations. Coordinating an effort to develop and implement novel solutions to global poverty isn't something that can be done at a grassroots level in one community. Consider running idea management software or a crowdsourcing initiative. Set up one campaign or project for each problem or issue area encompassed by that broader goal. Are you trying to coordinate neighborhood groups' efforts at getting more and better city parks? That sort of project clearly just calls for "old-fashioned" collaboration by meeting and conference call. To get really fancy this coalition could set up a list serve or a mailing list.

Evaluating Ideas

The time to decide what counts as a good idea comes before you need to implement the idea. Now is the time to decide what counts as a good idea. The criteria will be based on time, money, talent, staff, volunteers, and the social environment. Goals and objectives are important considerations because they determine the sorts of ideas that can move the organization forward. The culture, politics, laws, demographics, and economic conditions that exist when the ideas are implemented need to be accounted for in creating evaluation criteria. An intuitive and informal process is not necessarily bad – you presumably know your subject quite well. An informal process is still inferior because it informal evaluations allow too much room for subjective considerations and for important considerations to be missed.

Consider the time and money to be invested in implementing this idea. A snap judgment that the idea is a good one could waste huge amounts of time and money. A seemingly good idea can seriously damage an organization's reputation. Reputation is a sort of resource that needs to be considered in the idea generating stage, the idea evaluation stage, and the idea implementation stage of problem solving.

Selling Ideas

Depending on the organization's purpose this may or may not seem important. It is important. At the very least you need to convince coworkers that the idea is a good one. You may also need buy-in from volunteers, the board of trustees, or supervisors. Activists have to sell ideas to voters, politicians, school administrators, people who don't recycle, people who support the other side of an issue and et cetera. In almost all cases your plans will succeed to the extent that you can sell others on what needs to be done and why.

An important early step in social betterment efforts is to consider the audience(s) for your message. This seems straightforward and the point in this section is not to belabor the obvious. The point is to encourage a formal and systematic approach to the selling of ideas. Write things down. Brainstorm possible marketing tactics and strategies. Make sure you have thought comprehensively about what groups need to be sold on an idea and what benefits they will want or what arguments they will accept. There may be a need to learn some social marketing techniques that are beyond the scope of this book. Some people can learn on their own by studying a textbook, while others will need to take a class. Funds permitting, it would be wise to hire consultants.

The higher the stakes to the organization the more it makes sense to get professional help. You don't plan for retirement by simply assuming things will work out. Rather, you probably read expert advice or consult a financial planner. Review the basic marketing advice given in Chapter 15 and decide how it can be applied to those ideas and audiences you wrote down.

Recommended Reading

These books and Web sites give more information on the many topics touched on in *Creating Change.*

Solving Problems:

Altshuller, Genrich (1996). *And Suddenly the Inventor Appeared: TRIZ. The Theory of Inventive Problem Solving.* Worcester, MA: Technical Innovation Center.

Buzan, Tony (1991). *Use Both Sides of Your Brain: New Mind-Mapping Techniques.* New York: Penguin Books.

De Bono, Edward. (2000). *New Thinking for the New Millennium.* Beverly Hills, CA: New Millennium Press.

De Bono, Edward (1992). *Serious Creativity: Using the Power of Lateral Thinking to Create New Ideas.* New York: HarperCollins.

Jones, Morgan (1998).*The Thinker's Toolkit.* New York: Three Rivers Press.

Kepner, Charles and Benjamin Tregoe (1997). *The New Rational Manager.* Princeton, NJ: Kepner-Tregoe.

McCoy, Chalres W. (2002). *Why Didn't I Think of That? Think the Unthinkable and Achieve Creative Greatness.* New York: Prentice Hall.

Schwartz, Peter (1996). *The Art of the Long View: Planning for the Future in an Uncertain World.* New York: Currency.

Generating Ideas:

Fobes, Richard (1993). *The Creative Problem Solver's Toolkit.* Portland, OR: Solutions Through Innovation.

Michalko, Michael (1999). *Cracking Creativity: The Secrets of Creative Genius.* Berkeley, CA: Ten Speed Press.

Michalko, Michael (1991). *Thinkertoys: A Handbook of Business Creativity for the 1990s.* Berkeley, CA: Ten Speed Press.

Thorpe, Scott (2000). *How to Think Like Einstein: Simple ways to Break the Rules and Discover Your Hidden Genius.* Naperville, IL: Source-books.

Selling Ideas:

Gladwell, Malcom (2002). *Tipping Point: How Little Things Can Make a Big Difference.* Boston: Back Bay Publishing.

Hall, Doug (2005). *Jump Start Your Business Brain: Scientific Ideas and Advice That Will Immediately Double Your Success Rate.* Cincinnati, OH: Eureka! Institute.

Veloso, Maria (2009). *Web Copy That Sells: The Revolutionary Formula for Creating Copy That Grabs Their Attention and Compels*

Them to Buy. New York: AMACOM.

Levinson, J. Conrad (2007). *Guerilla Marketing*. New York: Houghton Mifflin.

Rogers, Everett (2003). *Diffusion of Innovations*. New York: Free Press.

Andreasen, Alan (2005). *Social Marketing for the 21st Century*. Thousand Oaks, CA: Sage Publications.

Web Sites:

ThoughtOffice   brainstorming   software
http://www.ThoughtOffice.com
Imaginatik idea management software http://www.imaginatik.com
Concept mapping software http://www.nthdegreesoftware.com
Spark software http://www.ovoinnovation.com
The World Future Society http://www.wfs.org
Mind Tools brainstorming software www.mindtools.com
Creativity and Problem solving tools http://www.innovationtools.com
My site on social innovation! Www.chesterdavis.com

Appendix 1 – Social Innovation Examples

This appendix describes some social innovations that the author developed using the techniques described in this book. See if you can improve the ideas, evaluate them, or find ways to sell them.

Impact of Ideas Initiative

This is a research and analysis project inspired by ways to fight social pollution, an effort inspired in turn by a creative thinking exercise. Ideas that are are contradicted by the facts, illogical, or contrary to widely held values cost time and money. Activists especially might be interested in using the research results to attack their opponents, bolster their own claims about what needs to be done, or simply to publicize the extent of a problem that they care about.

The Impact of Ideas Initiative would be run as a virtual nonprofit organization and would distribute information through press releases, a Web site, and downloadable papers. Budget permitting, some newspaper ads or radio ads in some large markets might also be useful. A brick-and-mortar headquarters and a regular staff would be desirable. The main thing is to actually get to work with the resources at hand.

A tentative model for analysis would be to calculate costs in time and money by looking for data on the rate at which certain behaviors occur. Additional data on the time and money costs of certain policies and social programs would be used to identify the social costs of social pollution.

The Impact of Ideas Initiative would research both the personal consequences of social pollution and the societal consequences. How do we decide what counts as social pollution anyway? If people want to advocate for the traditional definition of marriage isn't that just their choice? Yes, but that doesn't make their choice a wise one. Anyway, family is a very important human value and the definition of what counts as a family is open to interpretation. A preferred form of family is just that, a preference based on ideology, religious belief, and custom. A century ago, an American man from the upper middle class might not have accepted the idea of a stay-at-home husband. Today, most Americans find the arrangement a bit odd, at worst. Norms about family life change but the value placed on a family does not change much.

Indulgences

Sometimes you find a great idea to steal. This idea was inspired by a now-forgotten television show that described this ancient practice of the Catholic Church. Catholic clergy used to sell time off from a parishioner's sentence in purgatory. You might want to buy some time off to make up for the extra days that some sin might cost. There were different limits on how many days one could buy from cardinals, bishops, and the Pope himself.

No, this idea isn't about the need to revive the practice of selling indulgences. Nor are we trying to get people to donate money as a way of making up for their bad behavior. I did have some such idea in mind. People could read a list of how much various sins "cost" them. It was really a tongue-in-cheek way to make people think about the real impact of their behavior on other people. For instance, breaking up with someone by email costs $10, while doing PR work for the tobacco industry would "cost" $3 million.

Bad ideas also cost us time. The same quiz could also show people the amount of time that they waste on activities that are illogical, unscientific, or that undermine human values. I'm tempted to ask about the time people spend reading tabloids or watching soap operas, but those activities aren't based on ideas that rise to the level of social pollution. Quiz takers could be encouraged to enter their hourly income so they can estimate how much their time is really worth. Someone who makes $20 an hour and spends 600 hours of time per year on activities associated with social pollution, wastes $12,000 a year. Plus, those 600 hours can't be gotten back. .

The idea of selling indulgences brings to mind two other ideas that might be more practical than getting people to pay, by charitable donations, for their misbehavior. Use the idea as a satirical way to remind people of the real costs of their misbehavior by running ads in whatever media can be afforded. Press releases could generate a little media attention for this rather strange consciousness-raising exercise.

Social Fact Finder

This idea was inspired by my search for ways to use the Internet to capitalize on my sociological background. I decided to use random input to generate some ideas. The simplest form of random input is to take out a dictionary, open it to a randomly selected page, and work with the first noun that's listed. I came across the word "sludge" and listed things I associate with sludge. This suggested something to clean up pollution in society.

Does this idea have any practical applications? In other words, what challenge is this idea really going to help anyone with? It does occur to me that it can be very hard to find relatively objective analysis of the causes of various social problems and the true magnitude of the problems. Maybe there needs to be a central Web directory for research, theory, and expert analysis.

Social Pollution Prevention

People make decisions about voting, finances, education and other important issues every day. The problem for society is that the decisions are sometimes based on poor thinking. The ideas we use to guide us are often illogical, contrary to known facts, or contrary to widely held values. And sometimes the decisions we make don't really serve our own long-term interests. The ideas that drive these sorts of decisions are social pollution – ideas, attitudes, beliefs, and perceptions that undermine values, are illogical, or are counterfactual.

Social pollution has personal consequences and social impacts. Those problems could be avoided if people were only taught to think differently about the significant decisions that confront them. Some of the consequences are quantitative and some can be assessed qualitatively. Voting decisions shape other political decisions, like decisions about spending priorities. A Congress dominated by social and physical conservatives will not spend money the same way that progressive Democrats would.

To the extent that these things are done according to illogical, counterfactual, or amoral considerations, social pollution is damaging society. Buying decisions, relationships, career planning, beliefs, and lifestyles are also influenced by the ideas we use to guide our behavior. Social pollution costs people time and money to the extent that illogical, counterfactual, and amoral ideas guide our decisions. This is something to be concerned about because the time people waste can never be reclaimed. The time and money wasted could be spent on things that would really bring people greater health, prosperity, and satisfaction.

Social Pollution

The introduction to this chapter hinted at the challenge or at least at a preliminary statement of the challenge: How do we educate people and motivate them to take action on changing the way they think? In other words, how do we motivate people to incorporate factual, logical, values-based thinking into their daily lives? Why this challenge merits attention is also mentioned above. Social pollution wastes huge amounts of time and money each year. The counterfactual and illogical ideas that undermine our values have to be countered somehow. Many activist groups, writers, and progressive journalists fight particular ideas in various ways. Those individuals and groups rarely attack the general spread of social pollution throughout society.

So, why focus on motivating people to use logic, facts, and widely held human values in their thinking? Why not focus on individual bad ideas in different campaigns, or just pick one idea and leave the rest to someone else? The answer to both questions is simple – equipping people to take care of themselves makes more sense than trying to address the individual bad results in a piecemeal fashion. That is not the most efficient possible use of time and money.

Why take on the ways in which people think and make choices? Why not tackle the sources of social pollution, which you haven't mentioned thus far? Social pollution comes from many, many sources. Television, radio, newspapers, magazines, the Internet, churches, schools, books, friends, coworkers, and family are all sources of social pollution. So, I think that answers the question of why there can't be one program aimed at the sources of social pollution. Consider an analogy with pollution of the physical environment.

If you want to reduce waste of energy in society, where do you concentrate your efforts? Maybe electrical utilities are a good target since there are so few of those companies and so many households. Consider that energy production suffers losses at the plant, in transmission, and in use by equipment in hundreds of millions of buildings and vehicles. Only a small percentage of all energy produced gets put to work by the end users. The rest is wasted as heat. Concentrating efforts on the end users makes more sense because the impact of a reduction is multiplied by the amount of waste that is avoided in the chain of energy production and distribution.

So, that takes us back to the original challenge. Exploration of the original challenge statement makes it seem reasonable to focus on the "end users" of ideas that have overwhelmingly negative consequences. We want to focus directly on those people rather than on the many diffuse sources of ideas, good and bad, that people encounter each day. Note that you could focus on one sort of idea, one area of social life (such as relationships – the single best area of focus in my opinion) or on a single source of ideas, such as television. Religion, education, television, radio and print media are already the targets of many individuals and groups. Why not focus on illogical ideas, counter-factual ideas, or on ideas that undermine our values? In each case we could easily find ideas that influence multiple areas of social life. So, why not focus on just one of the three? I think it is possible and desirable to focus on a set of new ideas or thinking tools, if you like, that can be applied across areas of social life and to all three elements of social pollution. This approach has the added merit, or so it seems, of not overlapping too much with the work of other individuals and other nonprofit organizations.

Where did this idea of combating social pollution come from anyway? I wanted to think of some way to use the Internet to capitalize on my knowledge of sociology. Random input seemed like an interesting brainstorming technique to try, based on what I'd read in Michael Michalko's book *ThinkerToys*. I decided to open a dictionary to a random page and use the first noun on that page as a source of ideas. The first noun happened to be sludge. Thinking of the characteristics and associations that go with that word led to two ideas. One was this concept of social pollution, and particularly to the idea that there needed to be some way of cleaning up social pollution. This nonprofit idea was one concrete idea. The other concrete idea, and the one that first suggested itself was to create a Web site that would help people find (relatively) unbiased analysis of social issues ranging from animal welfare to gambling to whatever else we could think of. The "social issue facts" site idea is described in more detail in Appendix 2.

This plan to fight social pollution sounds good on a philosophical level. What about practical action to combat social pollution? What can this organization, if there will be a formal organization, actually do? Will this be an online initiative or will there be real-world programs or projects? How do you know what counts as a good idea? Let's start by stipulating that this is a one-person show, with a shoestring budget.

Audience	Focus	Media
high-school students	logic	mail
voters	values	radio
college students	science/facts	Internet video
other young adults	defining social pollution	web sites
working poor	personal impacts	magazine ads
	social impacts	newspaper ads
	societal action step	
	personal action step	

To select a good option, we must consider the audience, the theme for our work, and the medium for spreading the message. The table outlines some possibilities in each category. Lastly, a good idea is one that can be implemented by one person on a limited budget.

The preceding table is nothing more than a graphical way to organize the options we have in each of the dimensions we are interested in. The table can be used to help us select a good option or options to pursue. So, what combinations make sense for a small-time operation that's only able to focus on one audience at a time? Some options, like using Internet video to promote anything to the working poor, can be dismissed out of hand. That possibility violates the rule that a good idea has to be one that lets us effectively reach a certain audience. Using direct mail to convince voters of the personal costs associated with making choices that are illogical, counter-factual, or undermine our values might be more reasonable, given a large enough budget. It makes sense to stipulate that this will have to be an online initiative, at least in the beginning. So, what can be done online to reach those audiences that can be realistically reached online?

Web videos on some aspects of social pollution – definition, sources, personal impacts, social impacts, and "countermeasures" (logic, science, values-based thinking) – could work. Videos are much more interesting than static web sites. Online advertising is probably too expensive relative to the expected results, at least for a one-person outfit. Viral video might work as a "marketing" approach due to the huge popularity of YouTube. The creative challenge involved in making an egg-headed subject appealing to college students (the main target for this effort) can be considered separately. For now, it is enough to have decided that using Web video to reach college students with a series of "social pollution prevention" methods makes sense. Any online strategy, especially one that offers some entertainment value, could obviously reach well beyond the original audience of college students in the United States. This fact makes the Web-based approach to public education even more appealing.

Appendix – Guide to Tools and Tasks

Working on this...?	Try this!
Looking for new ideas	Concentration
	Random Input
	Concept Mapping
Improving a program	Concept Mapping
	SCAMPER
Designing a program	Concept Mapping
	SCAMPER
	Provocations
Making a decision	Deliberation questions
	RICK
	MOST
	FIP, OPV, AGO
Studying a social issue	Questions, various types
	FiFo
	Thought Experiments
Planning an activism campaign	Phoenix Checklist
	Anticipation Questions
	Logic Bubbles
	Morphological Analysis
Program/project planning	FIP
	RICK

About the Author:

Chester Davis received his PhD in sociology from Oklahoma State University in 1999. Since leaving graduate school he has worked for a university, and for the federal government, in addition to making time for plenty of volunteer work with anti-poverty and environmental charities. Mr. Davis now works as a freelance Web writer and information marketer serving the nonprofit world. He lives in in Nashville, TN with two rescue cats. You can read more about his ideas on nonprofit marketing, social innovation, and social science at http;//www.chesterdavis.medium.com.

www.ingramcontent.com/pod-product-compliance
Lightning Source LLC
Chambersburg PA
CBHW060823220526
45466CB00003B/957